CLASSIC SHOTS

CLASSIC SHOTS

THE GREATEST IMAGES FROM
THE UNITED STATES GOLF ASSOCIATION

MARTY PARKES
FOREWORD BY ARNOLD PALMER
AFTERWORD BY THOMAS L. FRIEDMAN

 NATIONAL GEOGRAPHIC

WASHINGTON, D.C.

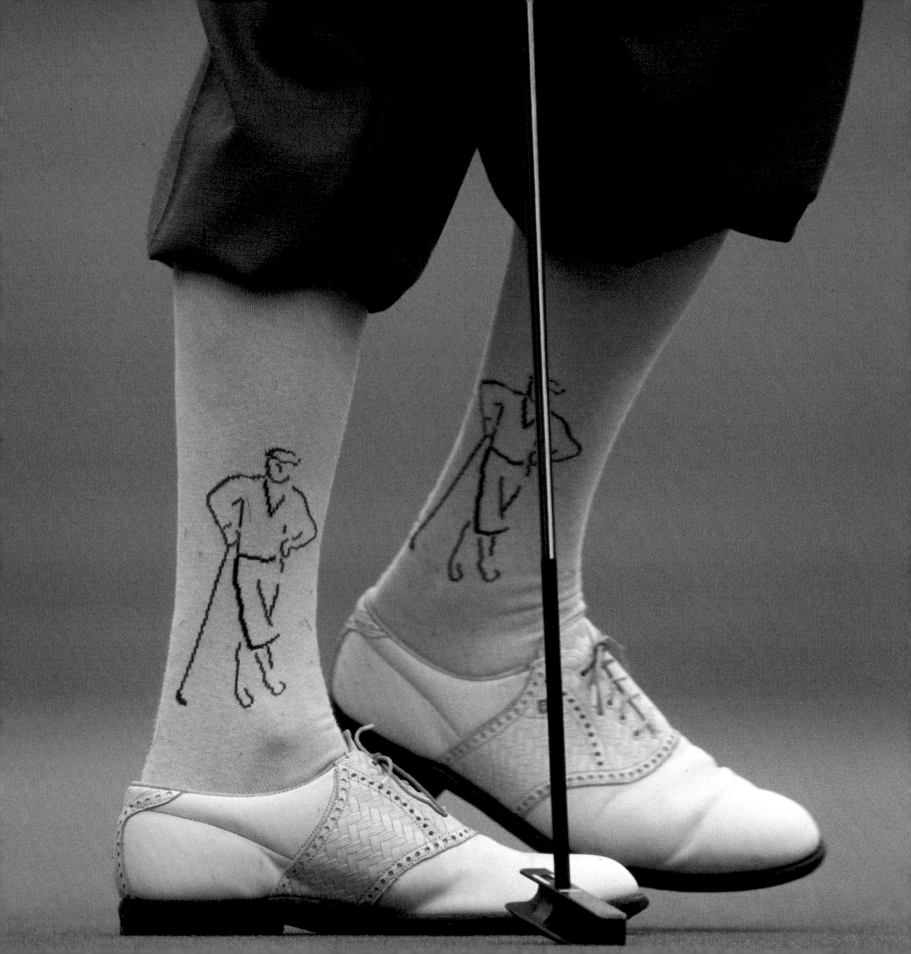

CONTENTS

(left) Payne Stewart's socks and shoes.

(previous pages) The 8th hole at Pebble Beach Golf Links
in Pebble Beach, California.

FOREWORD

Arnold Palmer

National Chairman of the USGA Members Program and longest-serving member
of the USGA Museum Committee

THERE'S NEVER BEEN A TIME WHEN GOLF WASN'T A MAJOR PART OF MY LIFE. Growing up in Latrobe, Pennsylvania, where my father worked as a golf course professional and superintendent, I spent countless hours playing and observing the game up close. The picturesque hillsides and undulating terrain surrounding Latrobe helped me develop an abiding appreciation for the inherent beauty of the game, its surrounding environment, and the turf upon which it is played.

THIS APPRECIATION for all aspects of the game allows me to express my admiration for the contents of the book you now hold in your hands. For almost as long as I've been involved in the game of golf, I've known about the organization created to protect and nurture it, namely the United States Golf Association. When I started to play competitive golf in the late 1940s in western Pennsylvania, I met several distinguished individuals who told me they served on various USGA committees. I didn't really know what that meant at the time, but it sounded like important and interesting work that inspired talented people to give of their time for no reason other than to keep the game of golf on a high plane. By the time I won the 1954 U.S. Amateur near Detroit, I had developed a more complete knowledge of the USGA and an ongoing admiration for what the organization does for the game of golf.

One of the many important functions performed by the USGA is to preserve the history of the game. Since the creation of its museum and archives in 1936, it has collected photographs depicting many of golf's most exciting or interesting moments. Through the years the USGA has gathered more than a half million images. The earliest were taken in the late 1800s and the collection runs right up to the present day. Some photos recount the accomplishments of the rich and famous. Others demonstrate outstanding play of the everyday golfer. Many feature only the pristine landscapes upon which the battles of our game are waged.

The USGA staff at Golf House has worked hard for more than a year in culling the thousands of images to select the best for this book. They vary by year, location, and venue.

But one trait remains common to them all. They all demonstrate the honorable traits of the game of golf while providing the opportunity for leisurely reflection. I hope you will take the opportunity to find a comfortable place to relax and enjoy turning the pages of this volume as your eye scans the many fascinating images contained here. There's even a photograph about a certain player who came from seven strokes back in the final round to win the 1960 U.S. Open.

Before I close, I would be remiss if I didn't mention how honored I feel regarding the USGA's decision to enlarge its museum and archives at its headquarters in Far Hills, New Jersey and name this addition The Arnold Palmer Center for Golf History. All of these exquisite photographs—along with thousands of books, films, artifacts and other items—will have a handsome new home. Such careful documentation and preservation of the game's history will allow many youngsters for years to come to develop the same deep, abiding admiration for the game of golf as I did those many years ago among the beautiful hills of western Pennsylvania.

Arnold Palmer celebrates his 1954 U.S. Amateur Championship at the Country Club of Detroit.

AN ACCIDENTAL COLLECTION

STRATEGIC PLANNING IS ALL THE RAGE THESE DAYS. It often appears that every organization has a long-term "strategic" planning process. This activity is touted as the answer to all ills, a sure-fire way for organizations to chart a clear path through turbulence and reach pre-determined goals.

This book represents the antithesis of the strategic plan. It's a volume that celebrates the incremental, the haphazard, and the anecdotal. It's the story of how the United States Golf Association amassed one of the finest and most substantial archives of sports images anywhere with little or no planning of any type.

WE'LL START OUR TALE of how this collection of photographs came to be with the beginnings of the USGA itself. The Association formed in late 1894 during a December meeting at the Calumet Club, which was located at 267 Fifth Avenue at the corner of 29th Street in New York City. In the first two decades of existence, the fledgling organization would not have a permanent headquarters. During this time, collecting and storing of anything would have been problematic. First and briefly during the early 1920s, it was located at 55 John Street before more permanent rented accommodations at 110 East 42nd Street were secured. The Association would remain there until 1935. The establishment of a permanent headquarters on 42nd Street with a sole employee named

(left) Gertrude Fiske, a leading Boston player, during the 1902 U.S. Women's Amateur at The Country Club in Brookline, Massachusetts.

T.J. McMahon, who served as executive secretary, provided the opportunity for displaying photographic images about the game and the USGA. At least two photographers stepped up and offered their services to help create a stockpile of images, many of which were used to grace the walls of the Association's headquarters.

One photographer was George S. Pietzcker from St. Louis, Missouri. "Photo" Pietzcker had documented many of the game's greatest competitions and competitors. He became one of the first professional photographers to specialize in golf. His work, in fact, appeared prominently in another volume published in 2005 by the USGA and National Geographic called *Golf's Golden Age: Robert T. Jones, Jr. and the Legendary Players of the '10s, '20s, and '30s* by Dr. Rand Jerris. This book chronicled stories and images of Bob Jones and his contemporaries. Pietzcker tirelessly traveled throughout the country during these three decades. He amassed a collection estimated at more than 15,000 golf images. USGA Executive Committee minutes from September 23, 1924 contain a suggestion from then USGA President J. Frederic Byers that the Association secure copies of photographs of past USGA champions from Peitzcker for suitable framing and display in the New York City office. The suggestion was seconded and approved.

During that same Executive Committee session, a letter received from another photographer, named Edwin Levick, was reviewed and considered. Levick lived in New Rochelle, New York, located just north of USGA headquarters. An accomplished writer as well as photojournalist by trade, Levick eventually abandoned generating words to concentrate solely upon producing photographs. His work encompassed a wide assortment of assignments: news, commerce and architecture, and sports, including golf. Although he became best-known for the large quantity of maritime images he generated, Levick petitioned the USGA to become its official photographer. The minutes note that this topic was discussed and subsequently dismissed: "after general discussion, it was decided that such designation would be contrary to the policy of the Committee." Perhaps the Association's close relationship with Pietzcker precluded a formal arrangement with another photographer. Many of Levick's images, nonetheless, found their way into the USGA's photographic archives.

Not much more is contained within the Association's institutional records about procuring photography for years thereafter. By the middle of the 1930s, though, the USGA moved again within New York City, this time to larger rented quarters at 73 East 57th Street. These more spacious offices allowed for the display of additional photographs. During this period of transition, a former newspaper man from Philadelphia named Joseph C. Dey, Jr. joined the USGA staff and replaced McMahon as executive secretary. As with so many other USGA activities during the next 35 years, Dey either played a first-hand role in the Association's policies or could identify the individual(s) who did.

Dey would later recount in the *USGA Journal* (February 1950 issue) how the Association first came to establish a formal museum in the middle of the 1930s. This museum sought to collect and organize items of historical interest, including photographs. USGA Executive Committee member George W. Blossom Jr., who would eventually serve as Association president from 1942–1943, visited the Biltmore Forest Country Club near Asheville, North Carolina in April, 1935. One day, while writing letters at a desk in the clubhouse, he noticed hanging on the wall above a framed invitation to a Golf Club Ball in Savannah, Georgia dated 1811, decades before the USGA's formation. Seeing this item convinced Blossom that the USGA should form a formal collection "to preserve and exhibit golf items of historical value, such as famous clubs, old golf balls, books, photographs, paintings, and medals." Blossom proved persuasive. Almost a year later, in January 1936, the USGA announced a plan to establish a Golf Museum and Library at its headquarters. Blossom would chair a Museum Committee designated to formulate such a facility.

LESS THAN THREE MONTHS LATER, the USGA moved to its larger quarters on 57th Street and the collecting began in earnest. It is interesting to note that the USGA museum became the first such sports museum in the nation, predating the National Baseball Hall of Fame in Cooperstown, New York by a couple of years. Another interesting historical note was that the museum's inception was undertaken during the USGA presidency of Prescott S. Bush of Connecticut, who later served as a U.S. Senator from this same state. Senator Bush is the father of the forty-first U.S. president George H. W. Bush and grandfather of the forty-third U.S. president, George W. Bush.

Given this mandate to collect items, a larger headquarters, and his ties to the press, Dey began to seek donations of photographs. "I don't know if this effort could be called an archive," contends long-time USGA staffer Frank Hannigan, who joined the USGA in the early 1960s and would serve as the Association's executive director during the middle of the 1980s. "Joe just sort of picked up stuff here and there. There was no USGA photographer, of course. My recollection is that he got a large collection of photographs from one source but I can't recall what that source was. But in general he just scrounged around. He had especially good relations with the media and he certainly collected images from them."

The photographs, it appears, were gathered as much for public information uses as for museum purposes. They would especially be used to illustrate stories in the Association's official publication *USGA Journal* that eventually came to be named *Golf Journal*. Hannigan recalls these photographs being filed alphabetically in folders without even a rudimentary card index system. According to Hannigan's recollections, "you just shoved your hand into the Js if you needed a picture of Bob Jones."

Bob Sommers, another long-time USGA hand who served as the editor of *Golf Journal* for more than two decades, echoed Hannigan's sentiments. "I don't remember anything about how the photographs came to be. There was never any discussion about it. They were just there …" Thus, with little planning, organization, "professional" expertise or physical storage techniques, the USGA's photographic archive was conceived and hurled into existence as an ongoing concern.

The USGA eventually moved to 40 East 38th Street in New York City in 1950, around the time of Dey's published reminiscence about the original creation of the USGA's museum. For the first time, the Association purchased property. The headquarters was an elegant 25-foot-wide, five-story, American-basement-style structure with a limestone facade. It came to be known as Golf House. After suitable renovations, it featured a section on the ground floor devoted exclusively to the museum's collections. The public was invited to visit and view the items. The price for the property and renovation totaled $100,000. Throughout the next two decades or so, Dey and others who joined him on the USGA staff continued to acquire black-and-white photographic images about the game.

One figure of note, Janet Seagle, increasingly brought some order from chaos after her arrival in 1963. Seagle became art editor of *Golf Journal* and assumed oversight of the USGA museum and its archives, including the black-and-white photos. In her customary take-charge fashion, she developed a more systematic way to file and catalogue them. Her involvement continued through many years and beyond her retirement from the Association in late 1989 and included service as a member of the USGA's Museum and Library Committee until her death on Christmas Day, 2003. A number of fine photographs that she took personally remain in the archives as well.

The Association would sell its 38th Street headquarters in 1972 and move to the rural landscape of Far Hills, New Jersey. The USGA successfully established its administrative functions on a former country estate of nearly 70 acres in a Georgian mansion designed by famed architect John Russell Pope as a private residence. Certain Executive Committee members envisioned construction of a golf course spanning the verdant property. This dream, however, never reached fruition. The museum initially encompassed one floor of the Pope-designed building. Later, as the organization grew, the museum completely filled the former home as the Association constructed other buildings among its headquarters complex to house its administrative functions.

Collecting quality photographs has continued as a priority during the Far Hills years. The black-and-white images were gathered together into a single room supervised directly by Seagle. The Association began to hire freelance photographers to cover USGA championships and events. *Golf Journal* shifted from a black-and-white to color format during the 1970s. These freelance shooters would capture their images on color slides and turn them over for safe storage at the headquarters. Diane Chrenko Becker joined the Association in 1983 and assumed oversight of the color slides while becoming art editor of *Golf Journal*, thus freeing Seagle to devote her full energies to the museum and its collections. Becker, like Seagle, also contributed some very good photographs until her departure from the Association in 1995. Nancy Stulack, still today a versatile and valued member of the museum staff, became supervisor of the black-and-whites upon Seagle's retirement. She learned to use a cross-filing system then in place to identify the location of particular images. The color slides and black-and-whites were eventually merged into one collection.

The USGA hired a fine New Jersey-based photographer named Robert Walker for a designated period of several months each year starting in the middle 1990s. Walker would fulfill the bulk of the USGA's photographic needs, with some freelance help as circumstances required. The Association hired its first full-time staff photographer, John Mummert, in 1997. Today, as the USGA's senior staff photographer and manager of photographic services, Mummert efficiently yet skillfully generates the bulk of USGA images with continued supplemental help from a variety of freelancers, Walker among them. These images are now recorded in a digital format. More than 10,000 a year are carefully captioned and catalogued and added to the archive.

To supplement this increased volume of photographs, the Association has added staff resources over time. Trained museum professionals joined the staff—dedicated solely to the photographic collection. Computerized filing systems and archival storage folders became standard. Research was undertaken to learn more about the background and/or subjects of the images. The Association constructed a storage room at its headquarters with proper climate controls to house the images in a suitable environment. Images started to be licensed on a regular basis to pertinent parties like commercial magazines, state/regional golf associations, golf facilities, and individuals. No one at Golf House today is permitted to stick their hand into any folder marked "J" to pull out an image of Bob Jones or anyone else without assistance and permission from the museum's staff.

THIS BOOK PRESENTS THE GREATEST PHOTOGRAPHS selected from among the more than one half million images that the USGA has gathered throughout its history. All 500,000+ were considered for inclusion. These images were reviewed carefully by a team of USGA staffers with assistance from a couple of National Geographic folks in an admittedly subjective search for the greatest among them. Another group of people might well have selected a completely or somewhat different group of photographs.

What criteria were used to determine greatness? To help answer this question, it may be useful to say first what this book is not. It is not a history of the game nor the USGA. Nor is it a

(following pages) Tommy Armour and his Marmon roadster.

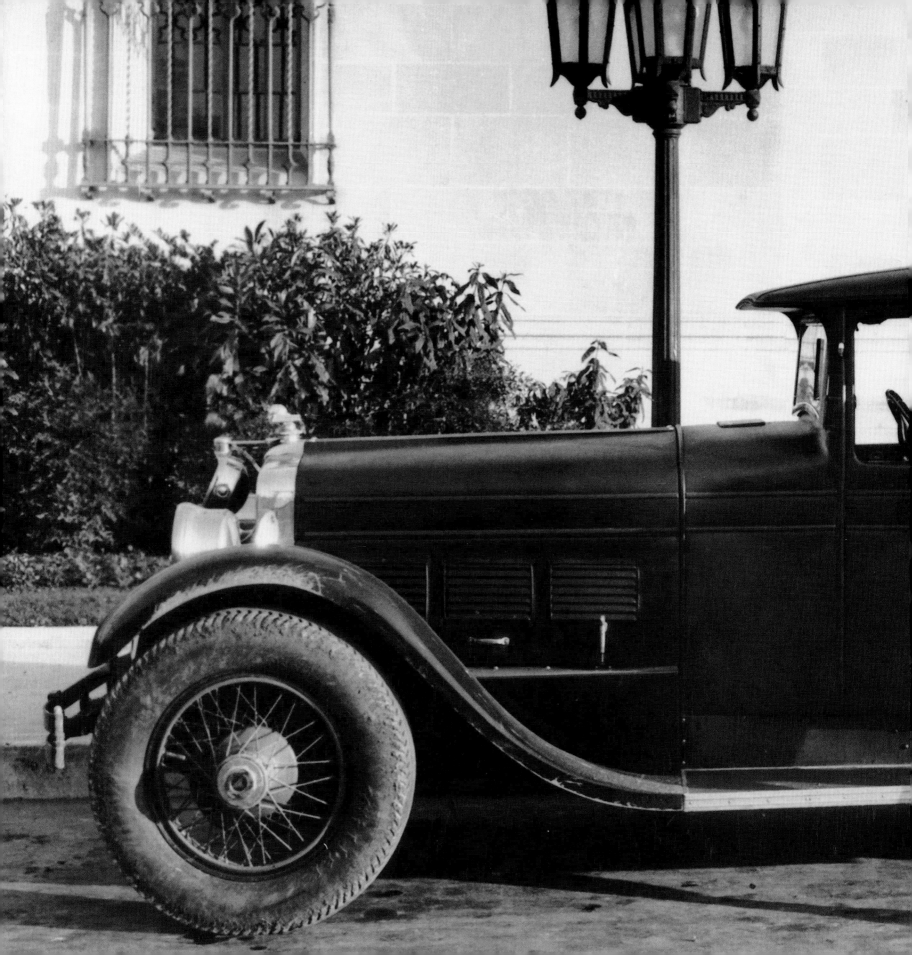

comprehensive chronicle of golf's greatest moments or players. There are certainly aspects of such elements contained in these pages. Some images document memorable moments in U.S. golf history. Others show casual scenes from this nation and overseas, especially from the British Isles. Some depict championship sites and moments, while others highlight portraits and personalities. Some images underscore the beautiful textures and hues of the game's landscapes and courses, while others showcase interesting artifacts and implements. But this volume is not designed to give an A-to-Z encyclopedic history of the game.

This book, by contrast, literally and figuratively presents snapshots from the game's annals. It attempts to celebrate and highlight the remarkable results of combining the artistic medium of photography with the history of one of the world's greatest and most widespread pastimes. It allows the reader to meander, offering continual chances to pause, ponder, and perceive. Jerris, the erudite and experienced director of the USGA's Museum and Archives, suggested that the rightful title of the book should incorporate an intersection of photographic and golf terminology, namely *Classic Shots: The Greatest Images From the United States Golf Association*.

It was easy to cull the more than 500,000 images to approximately 400. It became extremely difficult, though, to pare those 400 to the final photographs that, to use a bit of golf terminology, made the final cut. Part of this dilemma related to our inability to find a suitable structure for organizing the photographs. The most obvious way was to group by subject: championships, courses, champions, caddies. As the images were compiled, however, it became obvious that staring at a steady stream of the same type of shot, one after another, would dull their visual impact. A chronological treatment, alternately, wasn't feasible either. Although the final selections produced a complimentary blend of vintage black-and-whites and contemporary color photographs, we hadn't set out to ensure a smooth historical progression. There were, quite frankly, sequential gaps here and there. Some eras featured a rich and plentiful array from which to choose. Other times produced few, if any, images of interest. Since the goal was to select the greatest images without concern for historical progression, a chronological organization was rejected.

Once again, Dr. Jerris offered a solution. He advocated dividing the photographs into five geographic areas: the Northeast, South, Heartland (which describes an area that extends from Ohio to Colorado), West, and International. All but one prospective chapter would contain both black-and-white and color shots from all historic eras. The reader would be spared the tortuous task of leafing from one similar image to the next and, instead, enjoy a quirky mix of time frames, topics, and tones.

This geographic format helped us navigate and smooth the sometimes rocky path leading toward selection of the final photographs. A variety of opinions concerning particular images were expressed and debated, some with voices raised just a hint. Sometimes there were a handful of photographs of the same subject, which allowed for the selection of one and discarding of the remainder. Once again, though, emphasis remained upon selection of the most beautiful, interesting and technically-sound photographs—in short, the greatest images. It's important to note that even though we had agreed upon the geographic chapters, the images were not allocated according to region until after the best were selected. It was a happy accident that the division was as balanced geographically as it ultimately proved. This rather equitable distribution is really a testament both to the depth of quality of the collection and the widespread appeal that golf has maintained throughout this nation and the world over many decades.

The Northeast chapter features the largest number of images. This fact is not surprising since most of the oldest American golf venues as well as the USGA's headquarters are located in this region. The other four chapters each contain nearly the same number of images; most chapters feature more color than black-and-white images. The International Scrapbook section features all black-and-whites and contains a significant number of images from the British Isles. Some of these photographs have appeared in print through the years; others are showcased here for public review for the first time.

MANY OF THE IMAGES in this introductory section have interesting background stories that shed light on the times as well as on golf. For instance, the photograph on pages 14 and 15 shows a stylish and relaxed Tommy Armour, resting against a luxury automobile he had just been given after his victory in the 1927 U.S. Open. This would be the first of many Opens that would be contested at Oakmont Country Club, located in the suburbs of Pittsburgh, Pennsylvania.

Looking today at this image of Armour, it is hard not to reflect on the spirit of the era in which it was taken, a period that was memorialized as the "Jazz Age" by novelist F. Scott Fitzgerald. Armour, in fact, possessed some of the same traits of Fitzgerald's best known fictional character, Jay Gatsby. A decorated combat veteran of World War I who had witnessed some of that conflict's bloodiest fighting, Armour abandoned plans to complete his university education in Europe to seek his fortune in the United States. While Gatsby's troubles were the stuff of fiction, Armour's were all too real. Wounded in the war's first mustard gas attack during the battle of Ypres, he lost sight in one eye and had metal plates inserted in his left arm to repair severe injuries. Impaired vision and an injured arm are hardly attributes that an aspiring golf professional would want to have but Armour went on to pursue a golf career despite his difficulties.

This particular image was taken on June 22, 1927, by an unnamed photographer working for International Newsreel, a part of the Hearst media empire. It closely followed Armour's triumph over Harry Cooper in an 18-hole playoff at Oakmont by a score of 76 to 79 on June 17th. Its setting was just outside the palatial clubhouse of Congressional Country Club (itself a U.S. Open site) located on the outskirts of the nation's capital in suburban Maryland. Armour served as club professional at the time—having started a year earlier—and resided within the huge, impressive structure where he shared one-room quarters with his older brother Sandy. By 1929, about two years after his first Open win, Armour began focusing full time on participating in high-level competitions. His brother, and former roommate, succeeded him as club professional at Congressional.

The automobile that is featured so prominently in this image is a Marmon roadster. The members of the Congressional Country Club presented it to Armour in honor of his Open victory. Its price fluctuated in the neighborhood of $5,000 in 1927 dollars. Today few but the most committed automobile aficionados would even recognize the name "Marmon" but during the Jazz Age, it was ranked among the best vehicles on the road, on par (to use another golf term) with models from other celebrated manufacturers of the day such as Pierce Arrow, Peerless, and Packard.

The technical qualities of this image are striking. The carefully balanced juxtaposition of man, structure, and automobile, combined with just the right combination of natural light and human expression, place this image among the greatest photographs in the USGA archive.

Looking at the confident expression of Tommy Armour and the lush setting that formed his backdrop, it would be easy for a viewer who did not know the background detail to imagine that this young man lived life without a care in the world. Armour's personal sacrifices and the horrors of the Great War experienced by so many seem very removed. It seems impossible and implausible that just two years after this image was recorded, the Great Depression would spawn another calamitous era of despair and desolation. This downturn in national fortune would mark the end of the Jazz Age. By 1933, it would claim the Marmon automobile among its victims. One can appreciate this image of Armour all the more because it documents a truly tragic transition in American history.

WHAT IS IT ABOUT THE COMBINATION of golf and photography that produces such a potent partnership? Famed French photographer Henri Cartier-Bresson once coined the phrase "The Decisive Moment" to describe the underlying power of photography. The USGA's Mummert uses similar language to link this medium with the game: "It's that one moment in time. That's the magic. As a photographer, you get it all in golf. You see the beauty of the outdoors, pure and raw human emotion with each player competing against the golf course more than against one another. All these factors occur in an environment that's unpredictable and often harsh, which is what makes it fun and challenging at the same time. So much of golf photography is out of your control, dependent upon nature concerning light, temperature, and precipitation. At the end, in the simplest terms, you want to capture a striking, memorable image that impacts its viewers. And you want to do so in a way where you're proud to have your name appear on the photo but not in the story that accompanies it."

These days, photography in general—and golf photography in particular—commands an enduring popularity and affection among its viewers. Seeing a good photograph carries great importance. It can capture the essence of a person or place or event while transcending time better than any other medium. It can appeal to individuals from a diversity of backgrounds, ages, and geographic locations. It can demonstrate the vast array of human emotions: joy, exhilaration, disappointment, despair. It can make one vicariously feel sunshine on their neck, wind upon their back, or a pesky insect upon their forearm. It can reveal elements of detail that become obvious one moment and oblivious to the individual the next. And it allows the viewer simultaneously to experience several, competing sensations during the examination of a single image.

Doug Stark, the USGA's librarian/curator of archival collections, contends that the manner in which images are displayed also has a significant but sometimes overlooked effect upon their interpretation. "Part of the great charm of a photography collection like ours is that these images can be displayed in many ways. A single photograph can lead to competing stories told in varying ways. And how that photograph is presented in relationship to others affects its impact as well. There is no one single, correct way to display photographs. But the way they are displayed— whether hung on walls, printed individually, reproduced as a group in books such as this, or pasted into scrapbooks like so many in our archive—changes the way they are enjoyed and perceived.

(following pages) Dark skies loom over the 16th hole of the Orchards Golf Club in South Hadley, Massachusetts.

And when you begin to consider how to display a group of photos like we have here, you begin to notice where our collection is strong and where we have gaps."

DR. JERRIS OFFERS SOME FURTHER INSIGHTS about the golf/photography relationship: "Golf's beautiful landscapes lead to great photos. Each course is unique unlike the playing fields from most other sports, which have mandated dimensions. This variety of settings leads to a rich tapestry of textures and colors. Each course reflects the environment and surroundings of the venue. And all this environmental diversity is captured while still allowing the photographer the chance to show the human dimensions. They can profile the characters that have played the game and the implements they've used while doing so. Plus, think of the variety of types of golf photography available: picturesque landscapes, human portraits, competitive action, and inanimate objects. It makes for a challenging task for the golf photographer. But it also creates a nice opportunity for telling meaningful and enduring stories that transcend time and place."

Such apt thoughts lead to questions for the caretakers—the USGA museum staff—of the collection today. What images have been lost through the years? What should we be documenting today? What are we not preserving these days that we should be? What are we doing now to ensure that an expanded volume of these greatest USGA photographs could be produced a century from now? What unforeseen challenges will arise as obstacles to be confronted and overcome?

It is very fortunate that this collection of great images survives to the present day. Although the Association may not have had a master plan for the collection from the start, the decision of the organization to devote resources and spend time and energy gathering images and documenting the rise and spread of golf has led to an incredibly varied and rich archive. It is only, however, when these images are shared with others, like you, that their true meaning comes fully to life.

An iguana wanders across the 6th green while Ryan Moore putts during the 2004 World Amateur Team Championship at Rio Mar Country Club in Rio Grande, Puerto Rico.

THE NORTHEAST

(previous pages) The 14th hole at Newport Country Club in Newport, Rhode Island.

(above) Flags flew at half staff during the 2001 USGA Senior Women's Amateur to honor those lost on 9/11.

WHERE IT ALL BEGAN

THE NORTHEAST HAS PRODUCED MORE PHOTOGRAPHS in the USGA's collections than any other region of the United States. That's easy to understand when you consider that most of the first golf courses in the country were located here. Four of the five founding member clubs that gathered in New York City to form the USGA were situated in the Northeast. The Association has been headquartered in New York City or New Jersey throughout its history. Many of the most venerable national championship sites—with fabled names like Baltusrol, Merion, and Oakmont, to name three that have hosted a combined 45 USGA events through 2006—are located in this area as well.

This section's diverse photographs speak to the Northeast's rich contributions to golf as well as geographic diversity of the region. The photographs in this chapter range from charming black-and-white images, which have been taken at some of the sport's most historic locations, to vibrant full-color shots of many of today's outstanding players competing at a range of venues. Fabled golfers of the past, such as Francis Ouimet, Harry Vardon, Glenna Collett Vare, and Bob Jones make appearances as do some of the most accomplished players of more recent times, such as Arnold Palmer, Jack Nicklaus, Tiger Woods, Annika Sorenstam, and more.

(left) A group of professionals and their caddies at an early U.S. Open.

OTHER PHOTOS CAPTURE some of the game's challenging holes, such as the 6th hole at Newport Country Club in Newport, Rhode Island. Some photographs were included to depict the sheer natural beauty golfers often encounter as they play. We haven't forgotten the faithful crowds either; we chose some shots because we think they capture the emotions of the fans who attend USGA events.

Taken together, the USGA images presented in this section of the book provide a good representation of how golf grew in the U.S. from a curious import from Scotland played mostly in the Northeast to an international sport with increasingly sophisticated equipment, techniques, and courses. Right alongside as the sport grew, of course, was the USGA. To understand how the organization and this collection came to be, we'd have to go back to the 1890s during the USGA's beginnings—and a dispute.

The idea to form an Association arose over the question of who could designate a national champion. In 1894, both St. Andrew's Golf Club (Yonkers, New York) and Newport Golf Club (Newport, Rhode Island) staged invitational tournaments and declared its winner to be the national champion. Having two national champions, needless to say, created confusion. One player, a rather forceful character named Charles Blair Macdonald, had been in contention to win both competitions but captured neither one. Macdonald objected strongly to the ambiguity of the situation. Macdonald argued for the creation of a single national entity that could rightfully crown a truly national champion. At the same time, others in the sport recognized the need for an impartial national governing body to conduct national championships and oversee the interpretation of the game's rules and the rules of amateur status.

Delegates from five golf clubs—Newport, St. Andrew's, Shinnecock Hills Golf Club (Southampton, New York), The Country Club (Brookline, Massachusetts), and the Chicago Golf Club (Chicago, Illinois)—met at the Calumet Club in New York City on December 22, 1894. These delegates, including Macdonald, who represented Chicago, formed a nonprofit organization that would be run by golfers for the benefit of golfers. This new entity initially was called the "Amateur Golf Association of the United States." Each of the founding clubs pledged an amount not to exceed $50, which created a fund to defray expenses. Almost immediately, though, the founders realized that the Association would also need to address the needs of professional players. The name, therefore, was quickly changed to the "American Golf Association." Nearly as quickly, by the time that the by-laws and a constitution for the organization were adopted at the organization's first annual meeting on February 8, 1895, the group was renamed for a third and final time. It would now be known as the United States Golf Association, in recognition that Canadian golf fell under the auspices of the Royal and Ancient Golf Club of St. Andrews in Scotland.

NEWPORT'S THEODORE A. HAVEMEYER was elected as its first president, and he donated a trophy for presentation to the best amateur golfer in the land. This original U.S. Amateur Championship trophy, the Havemeyer Trophy, was destroyed by a fire in 1925 at East Lake Country Club in Atlanta, Georgia, where it was being displayed by virtue of Robert T. Jones's victory in the U.S. Amateur that same year. A replacement was given the following year by Edward S. Moore, the USGA treasurer. Although its physical characteristics vary significantly from the original, this replacement trophy is still called the Havemeyer Trophy.

Amateur competitions were more prominent in the USGA's early days than the professional game. Pros in this early era were considered to be of a lesser social status, mostly transplants from the British Isles whose foreign ways were often shunned by the New World elite. The first national championships were played in October 1895, at the nine holes of Newport Golf Club. This choice of venue, no doubt, reflected the influence of the Association's president. Of a field of 32 golfers, Charles Blair Macdonald emerged victorious in match play. His 12-and-11 margin of victory over the unfortunate victim, Charles E. Sands of St. Andrew's in New York, in the final match remains an all-time U.S. Amateur record.

The next day, on October 4, the USGA conducted the first U.S. Open. Bob Sommers, in his splendid history entitled *The U.S. Open: Golf's Ultimate Challenge*, provides perspective about the relative importance of these two early championships:

> *THE UNITED STATES OPEN BEGAN NOT AS THE MOST IMPORTANT COMPETITION in the game but as hardly more than an appendage to the Amateur championship, a sideshow that gave wealthy men the opportunity to gamble on what they considered the lower orders. While everyone acknowledged that the professionals were the best players, and the United States Golf Association was organized partly to conduct an Open championship, it was of secondary interest; the Amateur was the important event. Years went by before the Open surpassed the Amateur in the minds of the USGA and of the public at large.*

Eleven golfers competed in the first Open that day at Newport over 36 holes of stroke play (yes, they played the same nine holes four times in a single day). The surprise winner of the competition was Horace Rawlins, a 21-year-old English golfer who was serving at the time as an assistant professional at Newport. Rawlins scored 91-82—173 using a gutta-percha ball. Prize money totaled $335, and Rawlins garnered the first-place share of $150. This amount seems quaint compared to the millions being awarded today.

USGA national championships were by no means limited to men during that first year of 1895. The first U.S. Women's Amateur Championship was played on November 9 at Meadow Brook Club in Hempstead, New York. Thirteen women competed at 18 holes of stroke play. Mrs. Charles S. Brown (nee Lucy Barnes) of Shinnecock Hills won that first Women's Amateur with a score of 69-63—132. A silver pitcher had been hastily donated by two male benefactors to present to the winner, and Mrs. Brown's son, A.M. Brown, donated it years later to the USGA Museum's collections.

The Women's Amateur became a match-play competition in 1896 and has remained so since. In that year, Beatrix Hoyt, who was then only 16 years of age, captured the Women's Amateur championship. She added to this victory by winning two more for a total of three consecutive wins. She also became the first player to receive custody of the exquisite Women's Amateur Championship trophy presented by Robert Cox, a lawyer from Edinburgh, Scotland. This original trophy, still in use today, is the oldest survivor among USGA championship trophies and the only one donated by the citizen of another country.

The Northeast continues to have an enduring influence. Exactly 110 years after the initial presentation of the Cox Cup, the 2006 U.S. Women's Open was held for the first time at the site of the USGA's first national championships at Newport. The game and its leading competitions, however, are no longer the exclusive purview of wealthy and venerable private clubs. In 2002, the U.S. Open was held for the first time at a publically owned facility—New York State's Bethpage Black on Long Island. The event was such a success that the USGA decided immediately to return the U.S. Open to this course in 2009.

THE USGA PHOTOGRAPHIC COLLECTION captures golf's proud history and its many fields of play, but one of the unexpected pleasures of selecting the photographs for this book was finding snapshots of its hidden or forgotten recesses. The image of an unidentified golfer from the 1920s, which appears both on the front cover and on page 76 of this chapter, for example, certainly qualifies as a "classic shot." H.A. Strohmeyer Jr. of New York City, who is billed on the reverse side of the photograph as a "Photographer of Animals," shot this scene promoting Briarcliff Lodge, 30 miles north of New York City. This facility featured a fine golf course and Tudor-style luxury hotel that attracted the rich and famous of the day, including Franklin and Eleanor Roosevelt.

Other photographs highlight some unusally novel golf settings. The famed Merion Golf Club, located in suburban Philadelphia, for example, may be known for holding 17 USGA competitions, more than any other facility. But as the photograph on page 60 shows, it was also the scene of a memorable moment in the game's history, depicting one of the more challenging routes to a hole. In it 1930 U.S. Amateur Championship semifinalists Bob Jones and Jess Sweetser, along with several officials, are climbing down stairs located along the wall of an abandoned quarry to approach the 17th green. Not to be outdone in terms of topographical challenges, Shawnee Inn and Golf Resort in the photograph on page 56 features a bridge across the Delaware. The bridge was designed to be disassembled each autumn and reconstructed each spring to avoid damage by ice dams each winter. It remains in service today.

A number of delightful photographs capture golfers during some instantly recognizable and special moments in the sport. There's Taffy Bower at the 2005 USGA Senior Women's Amateur Championship as she guides the ball past the hole (page 54). Another, on page 49, taken at the 2005 U.S. Amateur, shows Jay Choi's method of guiding a ball out of a bunker. A recent terrific photograph of Phil Mickelson on page 64 conveys his dejection at letting the 2006 U.S. Open slip from his grasp. Another classic shot (page 36) shows a smiling Arnold Palmer at the 2002 U.S. Senior Open at Caves Valley Golf Club near Baltimore.

From the first strokes of the Apple Tree Gang in 1888 to Michelle Wie's booming drives at the 2006 U.S. Women's Open Championship, the Northeast has played a fundamental role in golf's rise to prominence. What follows are photographs from the collection that evoke the growth and vitality of the game, its players, and fans.

Bunkered at the 1996 U.S. Amateur.

(previous pages) George S. Pietzcker captured this scene during the 1922 U.S. Amateur at The Country Club in Brookline, Massachusetts.

(right) Phil Mickelson saves par at the 11th during the final round of the 2004 U.S. Open at Shinnecock Hills Golf Club in Southampton, New York.

(above) Arnold Palmer flashes his charismatic smile during the second round of the 2002 U.S. Senior Open at Caves Valley Golf Club outside Baltimore, Maryland.

(left) The final match in the 1963 U.S. Women's Amateur on the 13th hole at Taconic Golf Club of Williams College in Williamstown, Massachusetts.

(above) An early-morning, second-round match during the 2003 U.S. Amateur at Oakmont Country Club in Oakmont, Pennsylvania.

A competitor ponders his options during the 1965 U.S. Junior Amateur at Wilmington Country Club in Wilmington, Delaware.

The gallery at the 2005 U.S. Amateur helps Ryan Barnet search for his ball near a greenside bunker on the 2nd hole at Merion Golf Club in Ardmore, Pennsylvania.

Phil Mickelson during the final round of the 2002 U.S. Open on the Black Course at Bethpage State Park in Farmingdale, New York.

Quarterfinalist Bryan Norton marks his ball during the 2003 U.S. Mid-Amateur at Wilmington Country Club.

(previous pages) The 13th hole at The Apawamis Club in Rye, New York.

(below) Lee Williams plays out of the "Church Pews" during a semifinal match of the 2003 U.S. Amateur at Oakmont.

The sun silhouettes a standard bearer during the final match of the 2003 U.S. Amateur.

(right) During the third round of match play in the 2005 U.S. Amateur, Jay Choi escapes a treacherous greenside bunker on the 14th hole at Merion.

(below) Becky Lucidi blasts from a greenside bunker during her quarterfinal match in the 2003 U.S. Women's Amateur at Philadelphia Country Club in Gladwyne, Pennsylvania.

(right) A lofty perch for a member of the gallery during the 1929 U.S. Open at Winged Foot Golf Club in Mamaroneck, New York.

(below) A small gallery follows Findlay Douglas and Walter Smith during the final of the 1898 U.S. Amateur at Morris County Golf Club in Morristown, New Jersey.

A collection of signatures adorns a souvenir flag from the 2004 U.S. Open at Shinnecock Hills.

A massive gallery gathered around the 18th green to watch the final round of the 2004 U.S. Open.

(left) Taffy Bower's putt slides by the hole during her first-round match in the 2005 USGA Senior Women's Amateur at Apawamis.

(below) Jennifer Rosales celebrates a birdie at the 16th hole during the third round of the 2004 U.S. Women's Open at the Orchards.

The gallery at the 1938 PGA Championship crosses the bridge at the Binniekill, the famous 16th hole of Shawnee Country Club in

Shawnee, Pennsylvania. The bridge is taken down each fall to prevent winter storm damage and then reassembled in the spring.

(right) Nick Faldo plays his approach to the 17th green at Congressional Country Club in Bethesda, Maryland during the 1997 U.S. Open.

(following pages) Bob Jones and Jess Sweetser, with an entourage of officials, media, and security guards, descend into the quarry on the 17th hole at Merion during their semifinal match in the 1930 U.S. Amateur.

(above) Ed Furgol sinks the winning putt at the 1954 U.S. Open at Baltusrol Golf Club in Springfield, New Jersey.

Great Britain and Ireland's Hector Thomson, left, congratulates his American opponent, Johnny Goodman, right, following their battle in the 1936 Walker Cup Match at Pine Valley Golf Club in Clementon, New Jersey.

Meg Mallon embraces her caddie after holing the winning putt during the 2004 U.S. Women's Open at the Orchards.

A disconsolate Phil Mickelson on the 18th green at Winged Foot during the final round of the 2006 U.S. Open.

Six-time U.S. Women's Amateur champion Glenna Collett Vare possessed one of the most admired swings in the game's history.

Harry Vardon on the 3rd tee at Oakland Golf Club in Bayside, New York during his historic tour of America in 1900.

(left) Shinnecock Hills was one of the first clubs in America to build a course for the exclusive use of its female members.

(following pages) The 9th hole of the Longmeadow Country Club in Longmeadow, Massachusetts.

(above) The par-five 16th hole at Shinnecock Hills.

(above) Ruth Underhill, winner of the 1899 U.S. Women's Amateur Championship.

(right) Jack Nicklaus during the 1960 World Amateur Team Championship at Merion.

Contestants, including Harriot Curtis (foreground center), gather behind the 1st tee at an early U.S. Women's Amateur.

Three-time champion Virginia Van Wie leads the gallery across a bridge on the 5th hole during the 1934
U.S. Women's Amateur at Whitemarsh Valley Country Club in Chestnut Hill, Pennsylvania.

A nattily attired golfer of the 1920s drives from an elevated tee at Briarcliff Lodge in the Hudson Valley.

STROHMEYER.

*(previous pages) Deep bunkers surround the 17th green
on the Black Course at Bethpage State Park.*

*(above) The gallery heads toward the 1st green during the 1897 U.S. Women's Amateur
at Essex County Club in Manchester, Massachusetts.*

*(left) Francis Ouimet (crouching at left), lines up a putt on the 18th green at The Country Club,
Brookline, Massachusetts during a playoff for the 1913 U.S. Open.*

Construction of the new golf course in 1928 at Wampanoag Country Club in West Hartford, Connecticut.

Construction crews lay sod on the new greens at a course near Washington, D.C.

A huge crowd welcomes Retief Goosen, soon to be crowned champion, to the 18th green at Shinnecock Hills during the 2004 U.S. Open.

An early tournament at The St. Andrew's Golf Club in Hastings-on-Hudson, New York.

2006 U.S. Open Champion Geoff Ogilvy plays a delicate pitch to the final green at Winged Foot.

(right) James Sacheck and his caddie during the quarterfinal round of the 2003 U.S. Junior Amateur at Columbia Country Club in Chevy Chase, Maryland.

(below) Francis Ouimet and his 10-year-old caddie, Eddie Lowery, during the 1913 U.S. Open.

(left) Tiger Woods during the second round of the 2006 U.S. Open Championship held at Winged Foot.

(below) Natalie Gulbis on the 14th tee at Newport during the 2006 U.S. Women's Open.

(above) Michelle Wie tees off during a practice round for the 2006 U.S. Women's Open at Newport.

(previous pages) The 6th hole at Newport Country Club.

2006 U.S. Women's Open champion Annika Sorenstam drives from the 5th tee at Newport during the third round of the championship.

(left) Members of the Otsego Golf Club in Springfield Center, New York gather on the clubhouse porch.

(above) The Yale University Golf Team of 1900.

(following pages) The view from the tee of the 5th hole at Pine Valley, circa 1920.

TECHNOLOGY

TO ENSURE THAT SKILL REMAINS THE PRINCIPAL FACTOR in how well the game is played, the USGA tests balls, clubs, and other equipment for conformity to the Rules of Golf. The USGA performs these evaluations at its Research and Test Center in Far Hills, New Jersey. Thus, the purpose of the Rules is to protect golf's best traditions, to prevent an over-reliance on technological advances rather than skill, and to ensure that skill remains the dominant element of success for golfers everywhere.

CONFORMANCE TESTING The Research and Test Center receives nearly 3,000 equipment submissions each year. This includes nearly 900 different models of golf balls and more than 2,000 other pieces of golf equipment such as clubs, clubheads, shafts, gloves, tees and other devices. While the golf balls are submitted by a relatively small number of manufacturers from around the world, the other pieces of equipment may come from a major equipment manufacturer or a golf enthusiast tinkering in his/her garage. Regardless of the source, each submission is handled with the same diligence, care and confidentiality.

(left) Alexander Turner, Robert Crandall, and L.W. Crandall of the Burke Company in Newark, Ohio with a ball testing machine, circa 1925.

(above) Pulleys drive the belts that impart speed and spin to a golf ball in the USGA's Indoor Test Range.

GOLF BALL TESTING Manufacturers submit two dozen balls of each model to the USGA for testing. The Association's technical staff tests more than 20,000 golf balls per year for conformance using a combination of simple measurements and state-of-the-art testing devices.

Ball performance is tested according to the Overall Distance and Symmetry standards. Up until a few years ago, balls were tested by hitting samples outside on the USGA test range. Testing outdoors, though, produces less consistent results. Changing temperatures and variable wind and turf conditions make it difficult to evaluate balls under the exact same circumstances.

Today, we still hit each brand of ball with a mechanical golfer, but instead of hitting the balls outside, we hit them into a net in an inside facility and measure their launch conditions.

The USGA's state-of-the-art Indoor Test Range was designed to test golf balls year round. At left, the launcher shoots a golf ball through three testing stations with light screens. The ball's velocity and position are recorded and the data fed into a computer. This information is used to determine whether or not a ball conforms to the USGA's Overall Distance Standard.

off the clubhead (velocity, direction, and spin). We then use our Indoor Test Range (ITR) to determine precisely how each ball flies. The Indoor Test Range is a 70-foot-long "tunnel" through which the balls are launched using a golf ball launcher that is similar to a pitching machine. The ITR allows the USGA to measure the aerodynamics of a golf ball in flight. This information is used in a sophisticated computer program that accurately calculates driving distance of an actual drive. This "virtual" distance data is highly repeatable and not subject to weather variations.

Each ball is also carefully measured for size and weight. The balls are then tested to determine their initial velocity. All of this is carried out in a climate-controlled laboratory to make certain that all balls are evaluated at the same temperature and humidity.

GOLF CLUB TESTING All components of a golf club—heads, grips, and shafts—must meet USGA specifications. Tests range from the simple, such as water-displacement tests that measure clubhead volume to the more complex, such as a pendulum device that measures the spring-like effect of driving clubs. In all, some 2,000 clubs, club components, tees, gloves, and other equipment are tested at the USGA facility each year. The goal of all these tests is to keep skill front and center in the game that millions have come to love.

(left) A multiple-flash photograph of Bob Jones taken for A.G. Spalding and Bros. in 1939. The time interval between exposures was 1/100 second.

(below) A water-displacement test to measure clubhead volume.

THE SOUTH

(previous pages) Spanish moss hangs from majestic oaks on the Seaside Course at Sea Island Golf Club in St. Simons Island, Georgia.

(above) The Seaside Course at Sea Island played host to the 2000 USGA Senior Women's Amateur.

THE HOME OF LEGENDS

THIS SECTION OF THE BOOK includes the historic courses of the Commonwealth of Virginia, down to verdant greens of Florida, and as far west as Texas. It is a region that has contributed many important venues and individuals to the game's history. Year-round play afforded by the warm winter climate of the region has long attracted snowbirds from the North. The earliest courses were created to lure hotel guests during the winter, and this tradition of drawing resort visitors has spawned vast migrations of golfers that continues today. The excellence of the region's courses has long been established. Sites such as Augusta National Golf Club remain among the most fabled places in golf's annals. But the contributions of Southern states to the sport are not limited to great weather and great courses. This region has also provided a fertile training ground for a host of storied champions, from Bob Jones and Sam Snead to Texans Byron Nelson, Ben Hogan, and Babe Didrikson Zaharias. From its humble beginnings as an adjunct attraction for hotel guests, golf is now a way of life all over the South.

The spread of golf southward for the purposes of this discussion starts in the Old Dominion. Among the many historical sites in Virginia is The Homestead, in Hot Springs. Its Cascades Course has been the site of seven USGA championships. Across the state lies The Golden Horseshoe Golf Club at Colonial Williamsburg. Its layout holds the distinction of being designed by Robert Trent Jones Sr. and redesigned by his son, Rees Jones.

(left) Bicycles parked near the 12th green of the Long Cove Club in Hilton Head, South Carolina during the 2003 U.S. Women's Mid-Amateur.

Journeying southward to North Carolina brings one to the place that many consider the St. Andrews of America: Pinehurst. Located among towering pines and rolling sand hills, Pinehurst is a complex of eight golf courses, several of which were laid out by master architect Donald Ross. Although Ross is credited with designing many of the finest golf courses throughout the world, it is generally acknowledged that his masterpiece remains Pinehurst No. 2. Some of our finest images of the collection feature champions playing on this course. One favorite shows Payne Stewart rolling in his winning putt on the 18th green of Pinehurst at the 1999 U.S. Open (page 146). Stewart's pose is particularly memorable because he died tragically in a plane crash just months after this image was taken. Another moving image, this time of Michael Campbell, shows the champion pulling his cap down over his eyes to hide his tears upon realizing his victory at the 2005 U.S. Open played there (page 117).

Destinations along the coastline of South Carolina and Georgia have attracted resort patrons as far back as the establishment of Jekyll Island Club around the turn of the century. Its founding members included names like Morgan, Rockefeller, Astor, Pulitzer, and Vanderbilt. In more recent years golf has spread to the South Carolina meccas of Myrtle Beach and Hilton Head, which attract thousands of visitors every year. The latter now has an abundance of fine courses such as world-famous Harbour Town Golf Links designed by Pete Dye. Another notable Dye course is Long Cove Club, designed in 1981 and the site of the 2003 U.S. Women's Mid-Amateur Championship, its second USGA competition. One striking image in this section shows a magnificent egret that took a stroll on the seaside links (page 132).

Golf is a key resort attraction as you hop down along the barrier islands of Georgia. These scenic hideaways, featuring Spanish moss-draped live oaks, salt marshes, and sand dunes, hold opportunities for truly unique rounds of golf. One such club that has served as the venue for many USGA championships through the years is Sea Island Golf Club on St. Simons Island. A favorite photograph of ours shows the distinctive oak tree limbs framing the driveway leading up to the clubhouse (page 104). Not all the action is on the coast, of course. A short trip inland brings the golf pilgrim to Augusta National, the annual site of the Masters Tournament.

The spread of golf down into Florida can be said to have followed the railroads. One sepia-tinted photo (page 140) from the archives shows the inimitable Babe Ruth. While known for his prodigious drives in baseball, his passion for golf was, like so many of his attributes, huge. During his career with the New York Yankees, and for years thereafter, the Babe frequented golf courses in the state. This image shows the Babe following through his swing while attracting a crowd at Biltmore Golf Course in Coral Gables, Florida.

Another famous figure, this time from the world of golf, deserves special mention when discussing the Sunshine State. In 1991 at Bay Hill Club in Orlando, 15-year-old Tiger Woods became the youngest player ever to win the U.S. Junior Amateur, a feat he would repeat the next two years to become the only player to win three consecutive Junior Amateurs. He later won the U.S. Amateur at 18 years of age, making him the youngest player to win that championship. Woods built on these successes by becoming the only player to win the Amateur three years in a row, from 1994 to 1996. His first Amateur was captured at the Tournament Players Club at Sawgrass, on the east coast of the state.

Swinging around the hinge of the Gulf Coast, Alabama has created a delight for touring golfers called the Robert Trent Jones Golf Trail. The well-known designer was enticed to create 18 public courses, with 432 holes, at 10 sites all around the state. It puts a whole new light on the idea of a traveling band of players.

Any tour through the South must certainly include Texas. The Lone Star state is known for its many outstanding courses, such as Champions Golf Club in Houston, site of the 1969 U.S. Open and 1993 U.S. Amateur, and Fort Worth's Colonial Country Club, site of the 1941 U.S. Open and the U.S. Women's Open in 1991. The Colonial Club course is also known as Hogan's Alley, since Ben Hogan won five tournaments held there. In those years, he often competed against Byron Nelson, another native Texan.

That brings up another topic for which the South is justly famous. Some of the game's greatest players were born and learned the game here. One of the greatest of all time was Bob Jones, who hailed from Atlanta, Georgia. Jones won the U.S. Open four times and the U.S. Amateur five times. He remains the only golfer to have won nine USGA national championships and all four major championships of his era in a single season (1930). That Southern dominance continued into the middle decades of the last century. It would be tough to argue that Byron Nelson, Ben Hogan, and Sam Snead, who hailed from Virginia, were not the three best players of that period. All three chalked up enduring records of competitive achievement, although Snead was never able to capture a U.S. Open title. That prize eluded him throughout his career, despite winning more events on the PGA Tour than any other golfer in history.

IMAGINE HANDLING A GOLF CLUB so perfectly that the mechanical golfer the USGA employs at its Research & Test Center in Far Hills, New Jersey, is patterned after the motion of your swing? For Byron Nelson, it represents just one in a long list of accomplishments in tandem with the USGA, which includes his victory in the 1939 U.S. Open as well as his long years of service on the USGA Museum and Library Committee.

Nelson, Hogan, and Snead have all been the subject of special exhibitions at the USGA museum in Far Hills starting in the late 1980s. A permanent room dedicated to Ben Hogan was established with the permission and cooperation of his wife, Mrs. Valerie Hogan, in the summer of 1999. Mrs. Hogan personally assisted in the documentation and shipping of an extensive collection of her husband's memorabilia from Texas. Tens of thousands of golf fans have since visited this room, enjoying the exhibits highlighting the career of one of only four golfers in history to win the U.S. Open a record four times.

ON THE WOMEN'S SIDE is the Texan Babe Didrikson Zaharias. Winner of two gold and one silver medals in track at the 1932 Olympics, she showed the same flair for winning when she turned her hand to golf. She was known for her long drives, and these helped propel her to an unprecedented winning streak of 17 consecutive amateur competitions starting in 1946, including that year's Women's Amateur. She also won three U.S. Women's Opens in 1948, 1950, and 1954 before her premature death from cancer.

Finding photos of her, as well as other famous golfers, was one of the joys of combing the archives. One terrific shot captures Zaharias artfully chipping over a bush at Augusta Country Club in Georgia (page 143). Another depicts Snead slamming his way out of a water hazard (page 134). One vintage picture shows a young Horton Smith, who won eight times and finished runner-up six times in 22 PGA events during 1929, relaxing at Pinehurst (page 123). Perhaps the most remarkable discovery was a 1942 photograph of men in uniform putting on a practice green (page 114). The soldiers, stationed at Camp Gordon, Georgia, were the beneficiaries when the members of the nearby Augusta National Golf Club decided to assist the war effort in a novel way. Author John Strege recounts this tale in his fine book, *When War Played Through: Golf During World War II*, which received the USGA's Herbert Warren Wind Book Award in 2005. Strege wrote: "The USGA was willing to consider any idea that might enable it and its constituents to contribute to the war effort. One came from Bob Jones, who a few weeks after the (USGA's) annual meeting wrote a letter to new USGA President George Blossom Jr., informing him of Augusta National Golf Club's plans to build and maintain a driving range at Camp Gordon in Augusta, Georgia." They designed a putting green as well, built large enough to accommodate 75 players at a time. Adjacent to the green was a large, gradual slope that overlooked the practice range. It was capable of holding as many as 2,000 spectators for those occasions when Augusta National would conduct clinics for soldiers in uniform.

Many of the best images featured in this book resulted from careful planning and meticulous execution. Others, however, came about because a moment of happenstance, inspiration or whimsy revealed a scene worthy of capture. How could anyone plan Maru Martinez's enthusiastic reaction, after sinking a putt at the 2005 U.S. Women's Amateur Championship, held at Ansley Golf Club in Roswell, Georgia (page 127)? Who could not acknowledge the ingenuity of fans at the 2005 U.S. Open for creating some novel viewing areas (page 138)? Or perhaps we should not be surprised that one image from Pinehurst (shown below) contains a unique sundial for those golfers who like to monitor the time of day without the aid of a clock or watch.

Other photos were included for their ability to display the sheer beauty of Southern courses. The changing moods of the day caught a USGA photographer's eye on numerous occasions, such as the sun rising over the Holston Hills Country Club in Knoxville, Tennessee (page 120). Equally striking were the shadows thrown by players on the practice green early in the morning during the 2005 USGA Women's State Team Championship, held at Berkeley Hall in Bluffton, South Carolina (page 133). Another arresting image shows the shadows thrown by bicycles parked at the 2003 U.S. Women's Mid-Amateur at Long Cove Club (page 108). Such sights, captured in passing on the way to the next tee or hole, are part of what draws us all out to the course.

Once a refuge from winter, golf courses have expanded across the South. From the offshore breezes of the Florida coastline to the pinewood fastness of the Carolina hills, the region now affords splendid choices to resort visitor and daily golfer alike. The following pages offer a photographic glimpse into the wondrous variety that helps distinguish the Southern golf experience.

"Putter Boy," the famous sundial that has come to symbolize the Pinehurst Resort and Country Club in the Sandhills of North Carolina.

(previous pages) Servicemen stationed at Camp Gordon, Georgia practice on a putting green donated by the members of Augusta National Golf Club during World War II.

(right) The moment of victory for New Zealand's Michael Campbell in the 2005 U.S. Open at Pinehurst No. 2.

(above) Payne Stewart celebrates his second U.S. Open title after sinking a memorable putt on the 18th green at Pinehurst No. 2 in 1999.

(right) A heron stands guard on the bank of the Okatie River during the 2005 USGA Women's State Team Championship at Berkeley Hall in Bluffton, South Carolina.

(below) A final check of the 18th green at Pinehurst No. 2 on the morning of the first round of the 2005 U.S. Open.

(above) The Southern Golf Association's Olympic Cup Team of 1920, including, from left to right, Bob Jones, Pollock Boyd, Perry Adair, and Tom Prescott.

(previous pages) The 16th hole at Holston Hills Country Club in Knoxville, Tennessee.

(above) Portrait of accomplished professional Horton Smith, taken in Pinehurst, North Carolina during the late 1920s.

(following pages) The 17th hole at Atlanta Athletic Club in Duluth, Georgia.

Jason Gore birdies the final hole to complete his third round in the 2005 U.S. Open.

Maru Martinez sinks a long putt on the 8th hole during the final
of the 2005 U.S. Women's Amateur at Ansley Golf Club in Roswell, Georgia.

(right) Fans in the grandstand near the 16th green turn to watch Retief Goosen drive from the 17th tee in the third round of the 2005 U.S. Open.

(below) Stately pines line the fairways at Pinehurst No. 2.

(previous pages) Phil Mickelson's caddie approaches the 10th green during the third round of the 2005 U.S. Open.

(right) Lights illuminate early morning practice on the putting green at Berkeley Hall during the 2005 USGA Women's State Team Championship.

(above) The gallery following the 2003 U.S. Women's Mid-Amateur at Long Cove Club on Hilton Head included this Great Egret.

(left) A photographer may have posed Virginia's legendary sweet-swinger, Sam Snead, in an unlikely position, but the results were stunning.

(below) Atlanta's Charlie Yates blasts from a bunker during the 1936 Western Amateur.

The morning sun rises over the 18th green during the 2005 U.S. Open.

A few members of the gallery exercised some creativity to gain a better view of the action during the 2005 U.S. Open.

A member of Pinehurst's grounds crew removes dew from a green before the start of the 2005 U.S. Open.

A gallery gathers around the tee as baseball legend Babe Ruth slugs a drive at the Biltmore Golf Course in Coral Gables, Florida.

(right) Babe Didrikson Zaharias lofts her recovery to the 16th green of Augusta Country Club in Augusta, Georgia, during the 1950 Titleholders Championship.

(below) 1939 U.S. Open champion Byron Nelson learned the game as a caddie in Texas before rising to dominate professional golf in the 1930s and 1940s.

(above) A par putt clinches victory for Payne Stewart.

(previous pages) The 5th hole at The Farm Golf Club in Rocky Face, Georgia.

Golf balls were not the only objects in flight during the 2000 USGA Senior Women's Amateur at Sea Island.

(right) The 10th hole at Pine Needles Golf Resort meanders through the stately forest of Southern Pines, North Carolina.

(following pages) The 10th hole on the Seaside Course at Sea Island.

(below) Sprinklers at sunrise.

Roughing It

NEARLY TWO-THIRDS OF THE ACREAGE OF MOST GOLF COURSES is comprised of rough or naturalized areas that harbor a surprising diversity of wildlife. As golf has become more popular, people have become increasingly interested in how golf affects land resources and wildlife. Many golf organizations, led by the USGA, have actively sought to answer questions about the ongoing relationship between golf and its surrounding environment. Toward this end, the USGA has supported university studies and research projects to evaluate these issues. Two programs that have enjoyed consistent, long-time USGA support are the Audubon Cooperative Sanctuary Program for Golf Courses and another initiative called Wildlife Links.

THE AUDUBON COOPERATIVE SANCTUARY PROGRAM FOR GOLF COURSES (ACSP) was born in 1991 when a few hundred golf courses stepped forward to participate in a fledgling environmental education and certification program. With generous funding provided by the USGA, Audubon International crafted a program to address golf's environmental concerns and take advantage of environmental opportunities. Today, more than 2,100 golf courses in 26 countries participate in the program, while an additional 129 golf course development projects

(left) An American goldfinch among the Black-Eyed Susans at Prairie Dunes Country Club in Hutchinson, Kansas.

(above) An American alligator guards the second hole at Berkeley Hall in Bluffton, South Carolina.

(above) A hailstorm transforms the landscape during the 1996 U.S. Junior Amateur at Forest Highlands Golf Club in Flagstaff, Arizona.

are enrolled in the Audubon Signature Program, which addresses environmental aspects of course development. More than half of those enrolled in ACSP have developed an environmental plan to guide management of their golf course. Of these, more than 500 have achieved full certification. Altogether, that represents more than 700,000 acres of golf course land, water, and wildlife habitats that are managed for the benefit of golfers and the environment.

Participating superintendents and golf course managers set the standard for the golf industry. Their successes have raised the bar for how golf courses can and should be managed. Consider these achievements:

OPPORTUNITIES FOR BIRD CONSERVATION are great and growing, and with more than 150 acres of open space on the average golf course, these layouts are primed to play an important conservation role. Researchers evaluate the special habitat needs of species commonly found on golf courses as well as those likely to take up residence with a little encouragement.

One study of 24 golf courses in South Carolina examined how breeding birds use a variety of golf course designs, from highly altered landscapes to those where the majority of native vegetation, including a substantial amount of forested area, remained intact. For each course, researchers noted the abundance of breeding birds, including long-distance migrants, as well as species diversity.

Not surprisingly, less-developed courses had a greater diversity of birds and migratory bird species, but other findings shed new light on which habitats provide the greatest value and in what amounts. The single most significant landscape attribute was the amount of forested area. But while the study confirmed the importance of maintaining large patches of native vegetation, it also revealed that disturbed areas can create vital habitat for some declining species that need the open, grassy areas golf courses provide.

SAFE HARBOR PROGRAM Another initiative with impressive results is the Safe Harbor Program run by the U.S. Department of the Interior. This program guarantees private landowners such as golf courses will not be subject to restrictions under the Endangered Species Act if they succeed in attracting threatened species to their land. An example of such work concerns a federally endangered species called the red-cockaded woodpecker. This seven-inch-long bird often nests in long-leaf pines—some centuries old and among the last remaining stands of such trees in the Southeast—that line adjacent fairways. The Safe Harbor agreement is helping the endangered bird battle back from the brink of extinction.

In the Sandhills of North Carolina alone, there are more than 90 Safe Harbor agreements supporting 56 groups of red-cockaded woodpeckers. Since the program expanded nationally in 1999, more than 320 private landowners protected 35 endangered and threatened species.

(below) Spider webs among the gorse at Ganton Golf Club in North Yorkshire, England.

THE HEARTLAND

(previous pages) The 9th hole at Rush Creek Golf Club in Maple Grove, Minnesota.

(above) A missed putt by Nigel Edwards means a loss for Great Britain and Ireland in the 2005 Walker Cup at Chicago Golf Club.

THE HEARTLAND

THIS SECTION OF THE BOOK COVERS a vast area of the United States' interior—from Ohio and Michigan, across the Midwest, and extending to the prairies and the Rocky Mountains. It encompasses Chicago, which was home to the sole founding member of the USGA located outside the Northeast. Since these courses don't fall in the traditional confines of the Midwest, we've called this section the heartland.

The epicenter of the game in this region has long been Chicago. Here, the region's first courses were created and the game first attracted devoted adherents. Its early prominence is due to one towering figure: Charles Blair Macdonald (page 201). Macdonald, whose role in the origin of the USGA is described on page 30, played a major role in promoting golf in Chicago and spreading popularity of the sport across the heartland.

Macdonald was an enormously colorful personality who proved to be a highly effective promulgator of the sport. Reared in Chicago by wealthy parents, he was sent to live with his grandfather in Scotland where he attended the University of St. Andrews. His grandfather was a member of The Royal & Ancient Golf Club of St. Andrews and introduced young Macdonald to golf. Charles Blair Macdonald was soon spending every moment he could spare away from his studies on the golf course.

(left) Ben Hogan signs autographs during the 1942 Hale America National Open at Ridgemoor Country Club in Chicago.

AFTER MACDONALD RETURNED TO CHICAGO in 1874, he endured nearly two decades of what he termed the "Dark Ages." Golf courses did not then exist in his native country. He made it his personal mission to introduce golf to Chicago. Eventually, in the spring of 1892, Macdonald was invited by his friend, Horace Chatfield-Taylor, to lay out a primitive, small golf course upon the lawn of the Chicago-area home of his friend's father-in-law, Senator Charles B. Farwell.

That same summer, Macdonald convinced others to join together to form the fledgling Chicago Golf Club, located in Belmont. He promptly laid out nine holes. The following spring, Macdonald devised an additional nine holes to create the first 18-hole golf course in the United States. The charter of the Chicago Golf Club was granted on July 18, 1893, with Macdonald as its most prominent member. The next year, he helped found the United States Golf Association. Macdonald would go on to become the first U.S. Amateur champion in 1895. He also became a skilled golf course architect who routed famous courses such as National Golf Links of America on Long Island, New York.

Macdonald was not the only Chicagoan to have contributed positively to the early days of golf. In 1916, another local competitor, Chick Evans, became the first golfer to win the U.S. Open and the U.S. Amateur in the same year. Only Bob Jones has repeated this feat on his way to winning the Grand Slam of 1930. Evans, like Jones, remained firmly committed to the concept of amateurism throughout his lifetime. Thus, he took the proceeds from his instructional phonograph records and donated them to the Western Golf Association, based in Chicago, and established the Evans Scholars Foundation. To this day these funds help provide college scholarships to deserving caddies, in whose ranks Evans once served while learning the game.

IT COMES AS NO SURPRISE that the Chicago area contains a host of superlative golf courses. Chicago Golf Club has served as the host site for 11 USGA competitions, including three early U.S. Opens in 1897, 1900, and 1911. Johnny McDermott became the first American-born player to win the national championship when he captured the final Open held there. South of the city is Olympia Fields Country Club, site of two U.S. Opens, most recently the 2003 championship. A photograph of Tom Watson rekindles the memory of one of the most remarkable first-day performances in the history of the championship (page 197). The 53-year-old Watson turned back the hands of time and rediscovered the skill he exhibited during his prime in the 1970s and 1980s. Yet it was his relationship with his caddie, Bruce Edwards, which most folks would remember long after the sun set that day (page 190).

The golfer-caddie duo has always remained one of the most recognized partnerships in any sport. Earlier that year, Edwards found he had trouble manipulating his fingers. Watson urged him to seek medical treatment. He was diagnosed with amyotrophic lateral sclerosis, better known as Lou Gehrig's disease. It is always fatal; there is no cure. The USGA, recognizing Edwards's plight, offered him the use of a golf cart, but he proudly refused. Instead, he walked the course beside Watson and carried his bag each step of the way. Galleries stood and cheered at each hole as the duo toured the layout. Upon reaching the 7th green, Watson stroked a 20-foot birdie putt. He directed it toward the hole as shown in the photograph. It stopped on the front lip, seemingly defying gravity as it appeared to hang only upon air. Then, as Watson approached, it toppled into the hole. The crowd erupted with a deafening roar.

Among notable public courses in the Chicago area are Catigny, site of the 2007 U.S. Amateur Public Links Championship, and Cog Hill, a mammoth complex of nine courses and site of the 1997 U.S. Amateur and three other USGA championships. It was started by local golf figure and one-time USGA Executive Committee member Joe Jemsek, who was determined to bring private club conditions to the public player. He succeeded handsomely.

Such dedication to golf can be found all over the courses in this region. Swinging out east would bring us to the player who amassed what is arguably the greatest competitive golf record of the 20th century, Jack Nicklaus. He grew up in the Columbus, Ohio, area, and learned the game at Scioto Country Club, site of the 1926 U.S. Open, won by Bob Jones. Nicklaus won his first competitive events at Scioto and moved on to nearby Ohio State University. While a student there, he won the U.S. Amateur in 1959 and 1961. He turned professional the following year and promptly won the 1962 U.S. Open, besting Arnold Palmer in a famous playoff at Oakmont Country Club near Pittsburgh and Palmer's hometown of Latrobe. During the next three decades, Nicklaus emerged victorious in an unprecedented 20 major championships (including his two Amateurs). He also collected eight USGA national championship titles. Only two players—JoAnne Gunderson Carner and Tiger Woods—have won as many, and only one player, Bob Jones, has won more (nine). During the 1960s, 1970s, and 1980s, few scoreboards at significant professional golf competitions appeared without the name of Nicklaus situated at or near the top.

Special mention should be made of another Ohio course, that of Inverness Club in Toledo. Of the four U.S. Opens it has hosted, the one in 1931 was the longest national championship ever played. At the end of 72 holes, Billy Burke and George Von Elm were tied at 292, requiring a 36-hole playoff. They then tied again and were forced to battle it out over an additional 36 holes. Finally, after 144 exhausting holes, Billy Burke won by a single stroke.

To the north, in suburban Detroit, lies another world-famous course, Oakland Hills. Designed by Donald Ross and remodeled by Robert Trent Jones, this has been the site of five U.S. Opens, including Ben Hogan's thrilling come-from-behind victory in 1951. Farther to the northwest is Crystal Downs, a formidable natural course on the rolling sandy bluffs along the west end of Crystal Lake near the shores of Lake Michigan, designed by renowned architect Alister MacKenzie.

SITUATED ON APPROXIMATELY THE SAME LATITUDE off to the west lies a second great Midwestern center of golf, Minneapolis-St. Paul. You might consider the entire state of Minnesota as mad about golf. According to the National Golf Foundation (NGF), it ranked first among all 50 states with a 27 percent household participation rate during 2005. Similar studies have estimated more than 730,000 golfers in the state. One reason for that is 90 percent of its golf courses are open to public play.

Minnesota has enjoyed a close relationship with the USGA through the years as well. It is the only state to serve as the host site of all 13 USGA national championships, the Walker Cup, the Curtis Cup, and the USGA State Team Championships. In all, it has hosted 34 USGA competitions. These events and their host courses have featured some important moments in the Association's history. Bob Jones, for example, won the 1930 U.S. Open at Interlachen Country Club in Edina, located just outside the Twin Cities, the year in which he captured an unprecedented Grand Slam of the four competitions then considered major championships. Hazeltine National Golf Club, located in the Twin Cities' suburb of Chaska, has hosted eight USGA championships. These include the 1970 and 1991 U.S. Opens, the 1966 and 1977 U.S. Women's Opens, the 1983 U.S. Senior Open, and the 2006 U.S. Amateur.

Minneapolis is also the birth place of one of the greatest women golfers in history, Patty Berg. She won the 1938 U.S. Women's Amateur Championship, one of 28 career amateur victories in a seven-year period. Generous to a fault, Berg's sparkling personality nearly overshadowed her talent. "People came to see her time after time, always laughing at the jokes, always admiring the crisp shots, and always loving Patty Berg," said fellow great Betsy Rawls (page 176).

Another frequent champion, JoAnne Gunderson Carner, is shown competing at a unique course in the region: Prairie Dunes Country Club in Hutchinson, Kansas (page 172). Carner finished as the runner-up to Barbara McIntire at the 1964 U.S. Women's Amateur. She had won this event on three previous occasions: 1957, 1960, and 1962. She would win it again in 1966 and 1968 before she turned professional. Her five victories trail only Glenna Collett Vare's all-time record of six. The photo (page 175) of Carner blasting her way out of a bunker hints at the unusual geographic features of Prairie Dunes and the distinctive vegetation that grows there.

Hutchinson lies not far from the geographic center of the 48 contiguous United States, 1,500 miles from both the Atlantic and Pacific Oceans and 700 miles from the Gulf of Mexico. It's hard to imagine, but thousands of years ago the waves of an ancient salt sea rippled across the region. This sea is now long gone, but its legacy of salt and sand remains in the rolling hills. The brown and yellow swatches of prairie exhibit undulating dunes, waist-high native grasses, and a palette of colors derived from many varieties of prairie flowers termed "gunch" without affection by the locals. These patches serve as a sort of Bermuda Triangle, condemning to perdition all golf balls unlucky enough to find them.

The western bastion of the heartland region sits a mile higher than the plains. Its most dramatic moment was captured in a famous photograph of Arnold Palmer flinging his visor skyward on the final green of the 1960 U.S. Open at Cherry Hills Country Club near Denver (page 170). In the minds of many golf fans, it transformed him into "The King," the commander-in-chief of a group commonly called "Arnie's Army" that has long been classified by some as the world's largest non-combat force. Palmer's chances for a comeback during the final round had been discounted by nearly everyone. Yet he attacked the course in his swashbuckling style on his way to a stunning score of 65. Palmer's rise to fame coincided with the ascension of golf on television. Seldom have a star and medium proved a better match. Palmer's good looks, friendly personality, and visible emotions won him the approval and affection of millions of fans coast to coast.

This is but a quick survey of the fine golf played in the interior of the country. The photos that follow, though, hint at the rich traditions that the sport enjoys here. Charles Blair Macdonald would be proud to see how popular his beloved sport has become in the nation's heartland.

Range balls at the 2003 U.S. Senior Open.

(above) Birdie Kim clinches the 2005 U.S. Women's Open by holing her bunker shot on the 18th hole at Cherry Hills Country Club in Cherry Hills Village, Colorado.

(previous pages) A singles match arrives at the 18th green during the 1969 Walker Cup at Milwaukee Country Club in River Hills, Wisconsin.

*A moment of frustration during the 1996 U.S. Women's Amateur Championship at Firethorn Golf Club
in Lincoln, Nebraska.*

(left) Arnold Palmer celebrates his victory in the 1960 U.S. Open at Cherry Hills.

(below) Gary Player begs divine intervention during the 1986 U.S. Senior Open at Scioto Country Club in Columbus, Ohio.

The 14th hole of Prairie Dunes Country Club in Hutchinson, Kansas.

(right) JoAnne Gunderson Carner blasts her way out of trouble during the 1964 U.S. Women's Amateur at Prairie Dunes.

(below) Patty Berg, the "Minnesota Spark Plug," claims the 1938 U.S. Women's Amateur at Westmoreland Country Club in Wilmette, Illinois.

(previous pages) Patty Berg autographs scorecards for some caddies during the 1938 U.S. Women's Amateur.

(right) Tiger Woods studies his line during the third round of the 2003 U.S. Open at Olympia Fields Country Club in Olympia Fields, Illinois.

(above) The late-afternoon sun surrounds Jonathan Hodge during the 2006 U.S. Amateur at Hazeltine National Golf Club in Chaska, Minnesota.

(previous pages) Michelle Wie drives for the Rockies during the second round of the 2005 U.S. Women's Open at Cherry Hills.

(left) A few members of Midlothian Country Club in Midlothian, Illinois during the summer of 1899.

(above) A moment to relax for J.H. Taylor, Fred Herd, and Horace Rawlins during the 1900 U.S. Open at Chicago Golf Club.

A gallery surrounds the 18th green at Oakland Hills Country Club for the conclusion of the 1951 U.S. Open.

Henry Liaw makes the putt during the 2002 U.S. Amateur Championship at Oakland Hills.

The afternoon sun proves challenging during the 1996 U.S. Women's Amateur at Firethorn.

(previous pages) A peek at the scoreboard during the second round of the 2003 U.S. Open at Olympia Fields.

(left) Tom Watson and Bruce Edwards during the 2003 U.S. Senior Open at Inverness Club in Toledo, Ohio.

(below) Arnold Palmer and his caddie on the 12th hole at NCR Country Club in Kettering, Ohio during the 2005 U.S. Senior Open.

(previous pages) A clean entry for Olympic diving champion Helen Meany at The Greenbrier in White Sulphur Springs, West Virginia.

(left) Tom Watson rips into a drive during the 1975 U.S. Open at Medinah Country Club in Medinah, Illinois.

(below) Tom Watson explodes from a fairway bunker during the 2003 U.S. Open at Olympia Fields.

Two-time champion Allen Doyle silenced the competition at the 2006 U.S. Senior Open at Prairie Dunes.

(below) A little body English and the putt falls for Tom Watson in the 2003 U.S. Open.

(following pages) The 8th hole at Whistling Straits in Kohler, Wisconsin.

(above) Chicago's own Virginia Van Wie claimed three consecutive U.S. Women's Amateur titles from 1932 to 1934.

(right) Charles Blair Macdonald, the "Evangelist of Golf," helped bring the game to the Chicago region in the early 1890s.

A crowd gathers as Carl Kauffmann and Milton Soncrant battle for the 1929 U.S. Amateur

Public Links title at Forest Park in St. Louis, Missouri.

(right) Jim Furyk birdies the 15th hole during the third round of the 2003 U.S. Open.

(below) Jenny Chuasiriporn searches for her ball during the playoff for the 1998 U.S. Women's Open at Blackwolf Run Golf Club in Kohler, Wisconsin.

Indiana's home-grown champion Mike Bell jumps for joy after winning the 2006 USGA Senior Amateur

at Victoria National Golf Club in Newburgh, Indiana.

Turn-of-the-century caddies and caddiemasters at the Onwenstia Club in Lake Forest, Illinois.

(above) Amateur short-wave radio operators receiving scores from the course during the 1937 U.S. Open at Oakland Hills.

(following pages) Bob Jones drives from the 9th tee at Interlachen Country Club in Edina, Minnesota during the opening round of the 1930 U.S. Open.

Jock Hutchison, Jim Barnes, Warren K. Wood, and Chick Evans posed with officials on the 1st tee at Olympia Fields

before their charity match to benefit the American Red Cross during the summer of 1918.

(left) The USGA's Mark Passey documents the 2006 U.S. Amateur at Hazeltine.

(following pages) The 17th hole at Whistling Straits.

*(above) Carter Rich, of the USGA's Research & Test Center, measures driving distances
during the 2003 U.S. Open.*

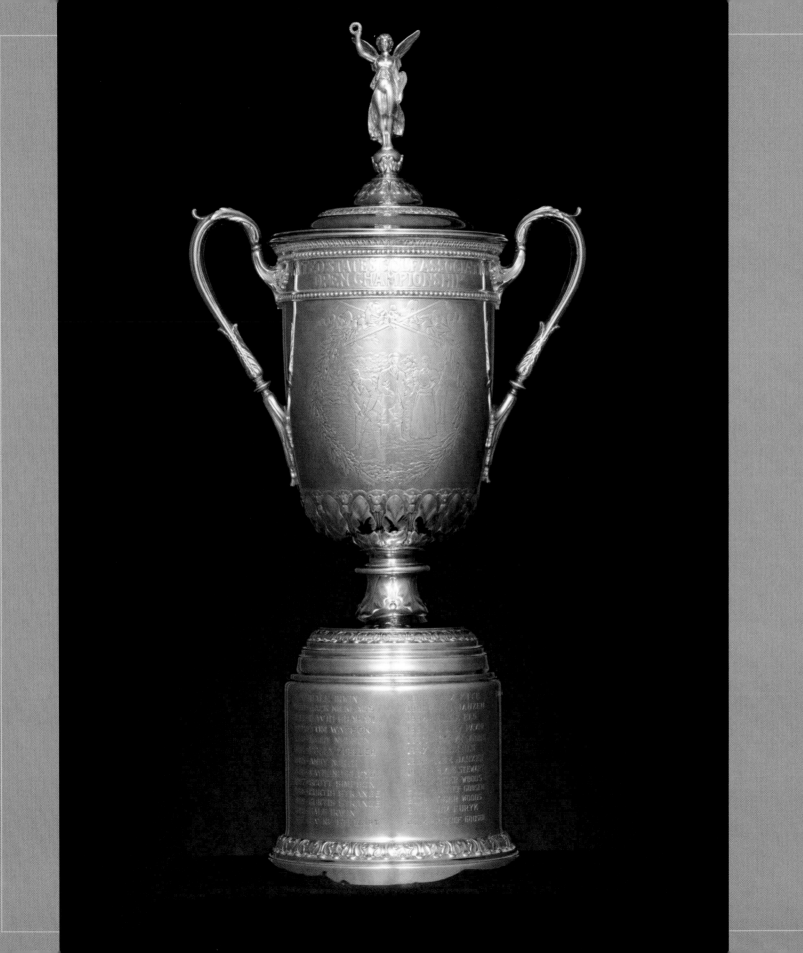

TROPHIES

HORACE RAWLINS WON THE FIRST U.S. OPEN CHAMPIONSHIP IN 1895 at Newport Golf Club in Rhode Island. As the victor, Rawlins earned $150, a gold medal, and custody of the sterling silver championship trophy for one year. The trophy was displayed at Rawlins' home club until it was presented to the 1896 champion. Thus began a tradition that has endured for more than a century.

The original two-handled trophy with its distinctive hand-chased golf scene was destroyed by fire in 1946 at Tam O'Shanter Country Club near Chicago. The USGA considered a new design, but opted to preserve the look of the original with a full-scale replacement in 1947. This trophy was passed from champion to champion until 1986, when it was retired to the USGA Museum. Today, the U.S. Open champion receives for one year a full-scale replica of the first trophy that was made in 1986.

THE WOMEN'S OPEN The "Ladies" Open was first conducted by the Women's Professional Golfers Association from 1946 until 1948. From 1949 until 1952, the Ladies Professional Golf

(left) The United States Open Championship Trophy.

(above) Jack Nicklaus receives the U.S. Open trophy following his victory at Pebble Beach Golf Links in 1972.

Ed Furgol cradles the trophy at the 1954 U.S. Open at Baltusrol Golf Club in Springfield, New Jersey.

Association assumed responsibility for the championship. During these years, the winner received a trophy donated by a fraternal order called the Spokane Athletic Round Table. The USGA declined the group's offer to continue sponsorship and instead provided a sterling silver, two-handled trophy produced by J.E. Caldwell and Co. of Philadelphia. This Women's Open Championship trophy was first presented in 1953 to Betsy Rawls.

The original trophy was replicated in July of 1992 by the family and friends of longtime USGA Committeeman Harton S. Semple. Semple, president of the USGA from 1973 to 1974, held various positions on the Executive Committee for nine years. Perhaps his proudest achievement in the game, however, was his daughter, Carol Semple Thompson, one of the top female amateur players in history. The Harton S. Semple trophy was first presented to Patty Sheehan in 1992 when the original was retired to Golf House.

THE SENIOR OPEN AND THE FRANCIS D. OUIMET MEMORIAL TROPHY Although the Senior Open is a comparatively new national championship begun in 1980, its trophy is the oldest of USGA's awards. On September 24, 1894, the Tuxedo Club of Tuxedo Park, New York, invited three other clubs to compete in the first American interclub tournament. Shinnecock Hills, St. Andrew's, and The Country Club of Brookline agreed to the challenge. While there is still some dispute as to who actually won, The Country Club team, comprising H.C. Leeds, Laurence Curtis, Robert Bacon, and W. B. Thomas, returned home with the trophy. The club retained the silver cup until giving it to the USGA for display in the museum.

In June of 1980, The Country Club suggested that the trophy be removed from exhibition and used instead as the formal award for the championship. The cup was presented "by The Country Club and Golfers of Massachusetts," and formally dedicated as the Francis D. Ouimet Memorial Trophy. Roberto De Vicenzo received it at Winged Foot as the inaugural champion. A replica of the trophy, complete with an engraving of the 1894 Brookline team, was produced by the USGA in 1997 and awarded to Graham Marsh at Olympia Fields Country Club in Olympia Fields, Illinois.

THE U.S. AMATEUR CHAMPIONSHIP AND THE HAVEMEYER TROPHIES The Havemeyer

• James D. Standish Jr., a member of the USGA Executive Committee, proposed the Amateur Public Links Championship in the 1920s, pointing to the swelling ranks of public course golfers. He donated the trophy for the event and it was first awarded in 1922.

• The Junior Amateur Championship Trophy was first presented in 1948 by the USGA. The large sterling silver bowl was produced by J.E. Caldwell and Co. of Philadephia. The trophy is a replica of a bowl produced by noted early American silversmith Samuel Williamson in 1796.

Trophies have been presented annually by the USGA since 1895 to winners of the U.S. Amateur Championship. The trophy was initially presented to the USGA on March 28, 1895, in honor of the Association's first President, Theodore A. Havemeyer.

The original Havemeyer, an ornate silver trophy produced by J.E. Caldwell and Co. in Philadelphia, was presented to C.B. Macdonald at Newport after his 1895 victory. The prize was then passed to each successive Amateur champion until November 22, 1925, when it was lost in a fire at the home club of Bob Jones, East Lake Golf Club in Atlanta, Georgia.

Rather than replace the original, the USGA decided to design a new trophy with an extended base to accommodate additional engraving. The new 18-karat gold, 16th-century-style steeple cup was produced by Crichton & Co. Ltd. of New York and formally presented in 1926

(left) Jack Nicklaus hoists the U.S. Open trophy at Baltusrol in 1980.

(above) The gold medal presented to Horace Rawlins for his victory in the inaugural U.S. Open.

Juli Inkster receives the U.S. Women's Open Trophy from Mary Capouch after the conclusion of the final round of the 1999 U.S. Women's Open Championship held at Old Waverly Golf Club in West Point, Mississippi.

by USGA Treasurer Edward S. Moore. A copy of the trophy was produced in 1992. It is this copy that is passed from champion to champion. In 1996, the USGA commissioned Garrard & Co. of London to replicate the original silver Havemeyer Trophy using two existing photographs.

THE WALKER CUP AND THE INTERNATIONAL CHALLENGE TROPHY In 1920, USGA President George Herbert Walker returned from a visit to the Royal and Ancient Golf Club of St. Andrews, Scotland with the idea to develop a regular competition between the two nations. Walker purchased a large sterling silver loving cup from Tiffany and Co. of New York that the press promptly dubbed "The Walker Cup."

The first official Walker Cup was contested in August of 1922 at Walker's home club, the National Golf Links of America in Southampton, New York. The U.S. team gained possession of the trophy, claiming an 8-4 victory. The matches were played each year through 1924, alternate years thereafter. Although the series of matches was interrupted by World War II, the international competition has remained a great success. George Herbert Walker, who served as USGA president in 1920, was the father-in-law of Senator Prescott Bush, the grandfather of U.S. President George Herbert Walker Bush, and the great-grandfather of U.S. President George W. Bush.

THE ESPIRITO SANTO TROPHY The Espirito Santo trophy has a long, circuitous history. The trophy first belonged to Nicolas II, the last Czar of Russia. After the Russian Revolution in 1917, the belongings of the Royal Family were scattered in auction sales. The Espirito Santo family of Lisbon purchased the trophy for use in a short-lived Portuguese international event. In 1964, the stunning cup was donated through the Portuguese Golf Federation to the World Amateur Golf Council for use in the new Women's World Amateur Team Championship. Originally a gold-plated trophy, the Espirito Santo was silver plated for its new use. Since France's victory in the inaugural WWATC in 1964, the winning team has received possession of the trophy for two years.

Tiger Woods shares the U.S. Junior Amateur Trophy with his father, Earl, following his victory in 1991 at the Bay Hill Club in Orlando, Florida.

THE ROBERT F. DWYER TROPHY The Women's Amateur Public Links Championship trophy was presented by Robert F. Dwyer in 1977. Dwyer was a member of the USGA Executive Committee from 1962 to 1974, and a member of the Public Links Committee. The sterling silver Robert F. Dwyer Trophy was produced by Gorham Silver in 1977. Kelly Fuiks was the first to receive it after her victory at Yahara Hills Golf Course in Madison, Wisconsin.

Pictured here are the USGA National Championship trophies (left to right). Front row: USGA's Men's State Team, U.S. Women's Amateur Public Links, USGA Women's State Team, U.S. Women's Open, U.S. Senior Open, U.S. Amateur,

U.S. Junior Amateur, U.S. Girls' Junior. Back row: U.S. Women's Mid-Amateur, U.S. Amateur Public Links, U.S. Mid-Amateur,
U.S. Open, USGA Senior Women's Amateur, U.S. Women's Amateur, USGA Senior Amateur.

THE WEST

(previous pages) The 11th hole of Pacific Dunes Golf Resort in Bandon, Oregon.

(above) Dr. Alister MacKenzie on a tee of his own design—the 13th at Cypress Point Club in Pebble Beach, California.

GOLFER'S PARADISE

THE WESTERN REGION OF THE U.S. offers the perfect setting and climate for spectacular golf. Known for having many of the nation's most scenic golf courses, the region has yielded more beautiful golf images than probably any other location on the planet.

Golf's growth in the West was helped by the completion of the railroads, which created boomtowns that attracted new settlers from around the globe. Among the newcomers were golf-loving Scots.

During the same year that the USGA was founded in New York City, Scottish employees of Balfour Guthrie, a financial trading firm, began construction of a golf course for the newly formed Tacoma Golf Club. University of St. Andrews graduate Alexander Baillie and another Scotsman, H.J. Bremer, routed the Tacoma layout using tin cans for holes. Baillie even arranged to have 30 sets of handmade clubs imported from Scotland. When the clubs arrived in customs, the bewildered Tacoma customs agent admitted the implements under the classification of *farm equipment*.

Soon the Tacoma club grew. In 1904, it moved to a bucolic site on the shores of picturesque American Lake, merged with a local summer vacation colony, and became known as the Tacoma Country and Golf Club. The club is one of the oldest private clubs west of the Mississippi and the oldest on the West Coast.

(left) Wesley Graham escapes the trees during the 2006 U.S. Junior Amateur at Rancho Santa Fe Golf Club in Rancho Santa Fe, California.

THE TACOMA COUNTRY AND GOLF CLUB IS TYPICAL of many of today's courses in the Pacific Northwest. The course features towering fir and oak trees and verdant turf that thrive in the region's damp weather conditions. When the skies clear, golfers are treated to the site of the majestic peak of Mount Rainier appearing on the horizon. The Tacoma course has seen many great players pass through, including "Long" Jim Barnes, who served as head professional from 1911 to 1914. Barnes would later win the 1921 U.S. Open. In its long history, Tacoma Country and Golf Club has previously served as the host site of three USGA women's national amateur championships as well as the 2007 U.S. Girls' Junior.

From its beginning in the Tacoma area, the game became popular throughout the West, eventually spreading as far as the Hawaiian Islands. Some of the region's courses have the heavily forested look of Tacoma. Pumpkin Ridge Golf Club, which is located outside of Portland, Oregon, for example, is situated at the base of the Cascade Mountains and features dense stands of fir trees. Its Witch Hollow course has hosted five USGA events, including the 1997 and 2003 U.S. Women's Open.

Several of the West's most picturesque golf courses take advantage of the Pacific's beautiful craggy coastlines. Some are reminiscent of the early courses of Scotland. Perhaps the best example lies along a remote stretch of Oregon's coastline, a complex named Bandon Dunes, where the United States team won the 2006 Curtis Cup Match. The complex is a fairly new addition to the golf landscape, having been developed and opened within the past decade. Many golf experts now consider the Brandon Dunes area to offer the closest thing to a true links course that the United States has yet produced.

There are, of course, venerable seaside courses in the West that have long enthralled golfers and photographers alike. One region rich with tradition is the San Francisco Bay area. A prime example is The Olympic Club, site of four U.S. Opens, including Billy Casper's startling comeback win over Arnold Palmer in 1966. On the public side is the nearby course at Harding Park, which uses the natural contours of the terrain to create a challenging layout. Just how challenging can be seen in one of our favorite pictures of W.C. Scarbrough Jr. blasting away on a severely uphill lie at the 1956 U.S. Amateur Public Links Championship (page 247).

THE TRUE MOTHER LODE OF WESTERN GOLF lies on the Monterey Peninsula, located a few hours drive south. This region, where the sea continually crashes against the coastline, features prominently in any collection of the best images of the game. Among a host of outstanding local courses is Pebble Beach Golf Links, which became the first public venue to serve as the site of a U.S. Open in 1972. Three other Opens followed, and another is scheduled in 2010. This famed course has welcomed four U.S. Amateur Championships as well as two U.S. Women's Amateur Championships and will host its first U.S. Women's Open in 2014.

Several of the holes at Pebble Beach are familiar to golf fans everywhere. Many of them are located along the rocky shores. Perhaps most famous is the par-3 7th hole, situated on a point of land jutting into the surf. It's one of the shortest holes in championship golf, measuring not much more than the length of a football field; it has been photographed, drawn, and painted from nearly every conceivable angle. One particularly memorable occasion at Pebble remains Tiger Woods' incomparable victory in 2000 at the 100th U.S. Open. He was the only golfer to finish under par for the championship, shooting a 12-under 272 to win by a record 15 strokes. It ranks as the most dominating performance in U.S. Open history.

Nearby lies Cypress Point, another golf course so beautiful that it has earned the moniker "the Sistine Chapel of Golf." While the course has fewer oceanfront holes than Pebble Beach, the 16th hole, a long par 3 over a bay to a green set upon a peninsula, is among the most photographed holes anywhere in North America.

Los Angeles is the scene of several of this section's vintage photographs showing Hollywood personalities. In one, U.S. Open champion Gene Sarazen and British Open champion Jock Hutchison provide advice on clubs to the silent-screen comedian Buster Keaton (page 259). In another, the famed swing band conductor Tommy Dorsey gathers another band, led by Byron Nelson, to help with his play (page 258).

Farther down the California coastline, just north of San Diego, lies another lovely seaside golfers' haven known as Torrey Pines. This public facility is comprised of two golf courses and is owned and operated by the city of San Diego. Torrey Pines will command the golf world's attention in June 2008, when it welcomes its first U.S. Open. It will join Bethpage State Park in New York as the only publically owned golf courses that have served as a U.S. Open host site.

Any discussion of Western golf also needs to include the many unique and inviting layouts carved within the arid deserts in states such as Arizona. Many of these courses are often attached to the region's many resorts. The USGA has had the fortune to use such venues as Desert Highlands near Scottsdale, Forest Highlands in Flagstaff, and Tucson Country Club for select championships.

The United States Golf Association Museum and Archives regards its photographs among its most important possessions. These images are treated with equal respect as the many precious treasures in our collections, such as paintings, sculptures, and clubs used by many of the game's legends. The earliest images in the collection were recorded upon fragile glass plates. Black-and-white film eventually replaced glass. Color slides gradually supplanted these. Today, digital images have made color film obsolete. All of these types of images have been used in this book.

MANY OF THE USGA'S EARLIEST PHOTOGRAPHS were once pasted into dozens of scrapbooks and photo albums that the Association now possesses. Some of the images that appear in this section on the West, as well as other chapters, were located in such hand-made volumes. Most of them were assembled prior to the Great Depression, and such heirlooms became treasured additions to the USGA's collections as the 20th century passed.

The USGA itself has helped this cause. Each year the Association presents all its national champions with a leather photo album featuring our best images documenting their victories. Based on the comments these national champions send back to Golf House, these albums immediately become cherished possessions. Such sentiments are expressed whether the recipient is a first-time winner or has captured multiple national championships during decades of play.

ONE VENERABLE IMAGE found among the USGA's many scrapbooks at Golf House is a photograph taken in 1925 of the 10th hole of Spokane Country Club in the Pacific Northwest (page 256). Francis X. Busch, Chicago's corporation counsel at the time this photograph was taken, owned this photo album. It features more than two dozen images taken during a memorable golf trip organized by *Golfer's Magazine*, a Chicago-based periodical first published in 1902.

How's this for a golf junkie's dream come true? Nearly 250 golfers from more than 30 states filled two special Pullman trains for a 5,000-mile golf tour of the Pacific Northwest. The trains departed Chicago on Thursday, July 30th and headed west. The caravan returned to the Windy City more than two weeks later on Sunday, August 16th. The complete cost for transportation, meals, and hotels for the 17-day excursion totaled the exacting sum of $264.37.

ONE REMARKABLE IMAGE is not so old. It was taken a few years ago before the final match during the USGA Senior Amateur Championship at Bel-Air Country Club in Los Angeles. It symbolizes the care and skill that has is expended in nurturing the visually striking yet varying surfaces upon which the struggles of our sport are played (page 255).

The majority of the activities that a golf photographer usually documents—and which spectators see—occur during play. But sometimes great opportunities for capturing quality images happen at other hours. This image shows a greenkeeper using a hand mower with delicate precision and evident care along the edges of a putting green. The long shadow that he casts speaks to the early morning hours long before play would begin that day. It's customary that several hours before the sun rises, the course maintenance crew of a host club like Bel-Air works with USGA championship staff to ensure that players encounter optimal yet challenging playing conditions expected at a national championship.

FROM MOUNTAIN TO DESERT TO SEASHORE, golf has flourished in the western region of the country, providing any intrepid photographer with a pleasing variety of choices.

Cutting holes for championship play.

(previous pages) A young Scott Simpson during the 1973 U.S. Junior Amateur at Singing Hills Country Club in El Cajon, California.

(left) A unique record of the 2003 U.S. Women's Open at Pumpkin Ridge Golf Club in North Plains, Oregon.

(above) A souvenir tossed into the gallery during the 1982 U.S. Senior Open at Portland Golf Club in Portland, Oregon.

"First Ball"—the 1st threesome of the 2000 U.S. Open drives from the 1st tee at Pebble Beach Golf Links.

Timothy McKenney watches the ball—but not his caddie—during the 2004 U.S. Junior Amateur at The Olympic Club in San Francisco, California.

1999 U.S. Amateur Champion David Gossett plays his approach through the fog to the 8th green at Pebble Beach.

(following pages) Play on the 9th green at Forest Highlands Golf Club in Flagstaff, Arizona, during the 2006 U.S. Mid-Amateur.

Four-time champion Jack Nicklaus during the 1972 U.S. Open at Pebble Beach.

Two fishermen pause as Bill Scarborough Jr. escapes the rough on the 16th hole at San Francisco's Harding Park Golf Course during the 1956 U.S. Amateur Public Links.

Ireland's Claire Coughlan plays from a greenside bunker on the 13th hole at Pacific Dunes during the 2006 Curtis Cup.

(above) Hale Irwin drops a long putt during the final round of the 1998 U.S. Senior Open at Riviera Country Club in Pacific Palisades, California.

(right) "Caddie Crossing" at Big Canyon Country Club in Newport Beach, California during the 2000 U.S. Women's Mid-Amateur.

(above) A pineapple marks the tee for Amy Spooner during the 1998 U.S. Women's Amateur Public Links at Kapalua Resort in Kapalua, Hawaii.

(previous pages) A remote camera captures a different angle on Irwin's putt.

A final cut for the greens before the final match of the 2004 USGA Senior Amateur
at Bel-Air Country Club in Los Angeles.

*(above) Byron Nelson (kneeling), Ralph Guldahl, and Paul Runyan (right) give a putting lesson
to famed orchestra leader Tommy Dorsey.*

(previous pages) The clubhouse and 10th tee of the Spokane Country Club in Spokane, Washington, in 1925.

Buster Keaton, one of Hollywood's early stars, shows his unusual clubs to Gene Sarazen (left)
and Jock Hutchison (right) in 1923.

(above) Tiger Woods drives from the 18th tee at Pebble Beach during the 2000 U.S. Open.

(previous pages) Andy Bean recovers from a hazard during the 2000 U.S. Open.

Hale Irwin's reaction to a missed opportunity during the final round of the 1998 U.S. Senior Open at Riviera.

Following a threesome during the 2003 U.S. Women's Open at Pumpkin Ridge.

(left) Philip Francis drives from the 11th tee during the 2006 U.S. Junior Amateur at Rancho Santa Fe.

(following pages) The USA's Paige Mackenzie drives from the 11th tee at Pacific Dunes during the 2006 Curtis Cup.

(above) Juli Inkster during the second round of the 2003 U.S. Women's Open.

USGA Museum

THE UNITED STATES GOLF ASSOCIATION MUSEUM AND ARCHIVES is home to the world's premier collection of golf artifacts and memorabilia. Founded in 1936, the USGA Museum is also the oldest museum in the country dedicated solely to sports. In the 70 years since the creation of the museum, the collections have grown to comprise more than 42,000 physical artifacts, a library of more than 20,000 volumes, more than half a million photographic images, and several thousand hours of historic film, video, and audio recordings. Together, these collections document the history and evolution of the game in America and around the world, including golf's greatest champions and most memorable championship moments.

THE USGA has long recognized and celebrated its role as the custodian of the ancient and honorable traditions of the game. Indeed, the USGA's constitution was amended in 1909 to include a description of the Association's caretaking role: "The Association has been formed and exists for the purpose of promoting and conserving throughout the United States the best interests and true spirit of the game of golf as embodied in its ancient and honorable traditions."

(left) The original Golf House, a brownstone located at 40 East 38th Street in New York City.

(above) The library of the original Golf House.

Highlights of the USGA collections include:

- Bob Jones' Calamity Jane II putter, medals, and personal scrapbooks from his Grand Slam victories of 1930.

- The scorecards and balls from the 1913 U.S. Open playoff between Francis Ouimet, Harry Vardon, and Ted Ray.

- Ben Hogan's vast collection of trophies, medals, awards, and clubs, including the 1-iron he used in the 1950 U.S. Open.

- Babe Zaharias' personal photo album from the 1954 U.S. Women's Open.

For almost 100 years, the USGA has seen the preserving, protecting, and promoting the rich traditions and history of the game as part of its mission.

GOLF'S TREASURE TROVE Over the years, the Association has asked the golf world to assist in collecting and preserving the history of the game. More than 2,000 individuals, including more than 220 USGA champions, responded by donating countless personal treasures from some of the game's greatest moments from its early roots to the present. In addition to these personal momentos of some of the game's most accomplished players are artifacts that speak to the game's widespread importance—items such as the modified soil-sampling tool that Admiral Alan Shepard used to play golf on the lunar surface in 1971 as well as the fragments of golf clubs and golf balls that were pulled from the rubble of the World Trade Center after 9/11.

These items reflect the passion for the game that every golfer feels. They are but a sampling of the history the Association has collected and displayed in its museum. Through these donations and the Association's own efforts at preserving and documenting the game, the USGA Museum and Archives has amassed an impressive collection that illustrates how golf has grown from a pastime of a few to a sport that has attracted millions of passionate participants.

GOLF HOUSE For more than three decades, a lovely Georgian Colonial mansion, called Golf

House, located in Far Hills, New Jersey, has provided public exhibition galleries, staff offices, and storage for the museum and archives. When the USGA moved to Far Hills from New York City in 1972, the museum occupied only the first floor of Golf House. Offices for additional USGA departments were situated on the upper floors as well as in the basement. Following the completion of a new administration building, Golf House was extensively renovated in 1987 and the Museum and Archives came to occupy all four floors of the structure.

Golf House itself has an interesting history. Noted American architect John Russell Pope had designed this building as a private residence in 1919 for a New York city financier named Thomas Frothingham. Pope completed many other private residences in the New York

Artifacts from the collection document the 1895 U.S. Open and Amateur Championships held at Newport Golf Club.

Spring at Golf House in Far Hills.

metropolitan area but he is perhaps best known for an impressive list of important public buildings. Among the most famous are the National Archives building, National Gallery of Art (West Building), Thomas Jefferson Memorial, Scottish Rite Temple, and Constitution Hall of the Daughters of the American Revolution, all located in Washington, D.C.

THE EXPANSION BEGINS Due primarily to the age and inadequacy of Golf House in preserving these collections according to modern climate-control standards, the USGA Executive Committee approved in February of 2005 a plan to renovate the existing museum and construct an addition of approximately 16,000 square feet to house public galleries, collections storage areas, and staff offices.

THE ARNOLD PALMER CENTER FOR GOLF HISTORY Perhaps the most interesting aspect of the new museum involves the name that will be associated with it—Arnold Palmer. A recipient of the Bob Jones Award, the USGA's highest honor, in 1971, and a member of the Selection Committee for the Jones Award since 1993, Palmer was the first man to win three different USGA championships: the 1954 U.S. Amateur, the 1960 U.S. Open, and the 1981 U.S. Senior Open.

"The King" breaks ground for the Arnold Palmer Center for Golf History.

Beyond his record as one of golf's all-time champions, Palmer's greatest legacy will always remain the way he played the game. His aggressive style of play and engaging personality captivated the public. His influence helped bring the game to unprecedented levels of popularity. One can make a convincing argument that Arnold and his plentiful "Army" of followers brought golf into the television era. Such exposure helped increase the number of players and golf courses dramatically across the nation. And as interest soared, so did the economic value of championship golf events such as the U.S. Open. The USGA has been able to increase significantly the services it provides to golfers through the years because of these burgeoning Open revenues.

So profound is Arnold Palmer's impact on the game, its people, and the USGA that he was asked, in 1975, to serve as the chairman of the USGA's Members Program. The first member he enrolled was none other than the president of the U.S. at the time, Gerald R. Ford. During the years of Arnold's leadership, the number of paying members has grown to more than 800,000 and Arnold's role as chairman has been responsible in no small part for the success of the program. Arnold has also served longer than any other member of the USGA's Museum Committee. In 1994, Palmer's career and contributions to the game were featured in a special exhibition at Golf House.

Because of the enduring connection that Arnold Palmer represents between all that is good about the game and the people who play it, the USGA has decided to name the new, expanded portion of its museum and library in Far Hills: "The Arnold Palmer Center for Golf History." An Arnold Palmer Room containing personal memorabilia from his private collection will be added to the facility as well. Never before has a USGA building been dedicated to honor a single individual; it is extremely unlikely that there will ever be another. The Association hopes this singular honor will remain a fitting tribute to the enduring relationship between Arnold Palmer, the USGA, and all golfers everywhere.

Architect's rendering of the Palmer Center designed by Farewell Mills Gatsch Architects of Princeton, New Jersey.

INTERNATIONAL

(previous pages) Driving from the tee at Murrayfield Golf Club, just outside of Edinburgh, Scotland, circa 1900.

(above) U.V. Stewart, of the Rolling Hills Country Club in Dhahran, Saudi Arabia plays an oil-slicked sand green.

INTERNATIONAL SCRAPBOOK

THERE'S AN OLD, ROMANTIC TALE IN THE ANNALS OF THE GAME that the first golfer was a shepherd who became bored with his work. To pass the long hours more quickly, he began swinging his crook at stones, knocking them into a hole in the ground. He became more adept with his crook over time, striking the stone greater distances over varied terrain. Rather than playing to the same exact hole time and again, he began to vary his route and map out a sequence of holes that he could loop around and play on a regular basis. Soon other shepherds took notice and began to use their crooks in the same manner to test their skills against one another.

While such tall tales are entertaining, the true story of golf's origins is far more difficult to pin down. It is certain that golf is not native to North America. Rather, the game was first transplanted here in the 18th century, and did not really take hold until the latter half of the 19th century. So where and when did the sport begin? And who were its first players?

The first evidence of any activity remotely resembling modern golf arises in ancient Rome. The Romans enjoyed a sport called *paganica*, which according to several accounts, pitted opposing teams armed with club-shaped branches to bat a feather-stuffed ball into their rival team's goal. But while *paganica* possessed some golf-like features, it's impossible to argue this game was the same as modern golf since, for one thing, the ball's destination was not a hole in the ground.

(left) J. Birnie Jr. drives from the 7th tee during the Cruden Bay Amateur Tournament in Cruden Bay, Scotland.

VARIOUS DOCUMENTS FROM LATE-MEDIEVAL EUROPE provide glimpses of other stick-and-ball games that bear characteristics that some associate with today's game. The French engaged in a pastime called *jeu de mail*. Played upon ancient roads bordered by high hedges, the players wielded clubs shaped like croquet mallets and whacked peach-sized spheres carved from boxwood. Their target was a raised pole located along the sides of the road. Once again, it contains some golf-like characteristics but cannot be considered a direct ancestor of the modern game.

A stronger argument can be made for a Northern European game known as *kolf*, which was played as early as the 1400s. Illustrations in several *Books of Hours* that were created in the 15th and 16th centuries depict residents of the Low Countries and western Germany using club-like sticks to strike a round ball on frozen canals or open fields. Delft tiles produced soon thereafter in Holland contain similar scenes. According to one popular theory, Dutch sailors carried the sport to the port cities on the east coast of Scotland. Here they transferred their game to the common links land, having found no frozen canals on which to play. All of this sounds great, but *kolf* later developed into an indoor game played on a hard floor 60 feet long and 25 feet wide. This area was bordered by walls two feet high that players could use to hit wooden posts placed at each end of the court. Thus, its evolution to an indoor game of mandated dimensions sets it far apart from modern golf.

During the early 1990s one scholar contended that golf originated in China before it was transplanted to Europe. Professor Ling Hongling, an instructor of physical education at Northwest Normal University in Lanzhou, China, claimed that an early Chinese game called *chuiwan* could be considered an early form of golf. The article contained a series of ancient line drawings that portray cherub-like figures waving implements that resemble golf clubs. These implements were used to drive a ball into each of a series of pits dug into the ground. Professor Hongling even presented a detailed analysis of how the clubs employed playing *chuiwan* resemble the implements utilized in modern golf. Most experts, however, were not persuaded that this ancient game had a direct connection to golf.

IT'S GENERALLY AGREED that golf first achieved widespread popularity in Scotland. Some scholars believe that the modern game may have its roots in a sport called *goff* that may have begun in Scotland around 1350. The first written reference to "golf" appeared more than a century later. The Scottish Parliament passed an act dated March 6, 1457, banning the game. The reason cited was that its burgeoning popularity was distracting the Scots to the point that they were neglecting to develop proficiency with the long bow. Such archery skills, in the government's view, would be more useful if the realm came under enemy attack than hitting a long drive. Like many law-abiding citizens of democracies henceforth, the Scots ignored this edict, along with subsequent ones passed in 1471 and 1491, and played through. Golf had developed a unshakeable hold upon the affections of the Scots.

The Scottish Parliament wasn't the only authority concerned about golf and its effect upon society. The Church of Scotland frowned upon the number of golfers who played the game on the Sabbath. Fortunately for these players, their sovereign, King James VI of Scotland (who later became James I of England and whose name is best remembered today for his version of the Bible), was an avid player himself. James VI announced that golf played on the Sabbath was acceptable as long as its participants had attended church earlier in the day. He subsequently appointed a Royal Clubmaker and, fifteen years later, an official ball maker who manufactured rudimentary balls made largely of leather and feathers, with a price limit set at four shillings by the Crown. Subsequent members of the Stuart dynasty enjoyed the game as well, most notably, Mary Queen of Scots. When she played golf just days after the murder of her husband, Lord Darnley, her detractors condemned her for being cold and indifferent to his fate.

THE SCOTS BEGAN BUILDING GOLF COURSES throughout the country. The narrow strips of sandy, treeless, undulating terrain that could be found along the coasts eventually became especially popular settings. The word "links" came to be associated with these seaside settings. Peter Davies, in *The Historical Dictionary of Golfing Terms: From 1500 to the Present*, defines "links" as Scottish in origin meaning: "rough, open ground; especially, a tract of low-lying seaside land of the east coast of the Lowlands held by a town as a common and used from the Middle Ages onward for sports, including archery, bowls, and golf. Such land is characteristically sandy, treeless, undulating or hummocky, often with dunes, and the typical ground over is bent grass, with gorse bushes." Over time, the word "links" became synonymous with golf courses located throughout the world—whether they were near a coastline or not. Particularly today, the term is commonly misapplied to refer to any golf course. But, many purists contend that to be considered a true, authentic links, a course should satisfy all the physical characteristics of the original Scottish definition.

The stretch of dunes alongside St. Andrews Bay became, over time, the focus of Scottish golf. A University of St. Andrews student named James Melville wrote in his diary in 1574 about golf being played there. A golf course was routed through a narrow strip of land bordering the sea. The course that eventually emerged featured holes situated end to end from a clubhouse to the far end of the property. One played the holes out, turned around, and played the holes in, for a total of 22 holes. The Royal and Ancient Golf Club of St. Andrews (R&A) was formed at this golf course in 1754. A decade later, several holes were deemed too short by the club and consolidated into longer ones. The total number of holes was reduced. If one played the holes out, turned around, and played the holes in, 18 holes would be completed. By the end of the 19th century, this number of 18 holes at St. Andrews became the standard for a "round" of golf throughout the world.

From Scotland, using the British Empire as a convenient conduit, golf spread to all regions of the globe including North America. It currently ranks among the most widespread and popular sports in the world in number of venues, participants, fans, and economic impact. According to some estimates, the game is played by more than 60 million people in more than 100 countries around the world. As one example of the game's global reach, the current roster of USGA member clubs, courses, and training facilities spans every continent except Antarctica.

UNLIKE THE OTHER REGIONAL SECTIONS of this book, "The International Scrapbook" pages were drawn entirely from the USGA's historical collection. The USGA sponsors international events and continues to add photographs from around the world to its collection. But in this section, we chose to highlight the early days of golf. These images capture the game's roots and its spread to sometimes unlikely places throughout the world.

As one might guess, the majority were shot in the British Isles. Golf's popularity in this part of the world, particularly Scotland, has long encouraged photographers to click their shutters. Just how enduring Scotland's influence has been upon the game is shown in its worldwide jurisdiction even today. While the USGA acts as the national governing body in the United States and Mexico, the R&A governs the sport throughout the remainder of the world. This continuing pervasive influence of Scotland underscores its standing as the cradle of the game.

This treasure trove of international photos allows us to trace the game all the way back to Old Tom Morris (pages 290, 297, and 298). One of the 19th-century pioneers of modern golf, he was a champion in more than his playing. His views on greenkeeping and deliberately placing hazards on a course have literally shaped the game we know today.

Among these sepia-tinted images emerges a host of early stars: Harry Vardon (page 298), J.H. Taylor (page 311), and James Braid (page 311) at the height of their powers. A truly distinctive moment was captured when Tommy Armour received his British Open trophy from a Scottish earl, complete with tartan kilt (page 314). Superlative women golfers were found as well, including Glenna Collett Vare with her 1936 Curtis Cup team (page 308). A later, whimsical shot depicts JoAnne Gunderson Carner posing in the type of rough no golfer would ever want to play—craggy boulders littering the seashore (page 291).

The portrait of Englishman Ted Ray (page 292) is striking. Most golf portraits taken during the early decades of the 20th century were staid and staged affairs. They usually featured a player clad in golf attire, standing ramrod straight and looking directly into the camera. A golf club often was placed in the player's hand in these literally still shots. Action portraits, in comparison, were a rare exception rather than the norm. And that's exactly what makes this image of Ted Ray so exceptional.

Ray's style of play is noteworthy. As Henry Leach wrote in *The American Golfer* of April, 1916: "He swayed his body, committed a number of minor crimes, and he used his enormous strength as much as he could … and so manages his timing that at the moment of impact he has all his skill, all his force and all his weight applied to the ball."

The photograph is shot from behind with Ray's face concealed from view. He's clenching a pipe between his teeth. His clothes are stylish, yet the flapping of the hemlines of his coat demonstrates the swirling force generated by the arc of his powerful, uninhibited motion. His right foot, in the follow-through position, reveals an early version of metal spikes that helped provide the delicate physical balance in executing such a forceful swing.

Not all of the images displayed in the international section are confined to the British Isles. Intrepid colonizers spread the game everywhere. One locale was Egypt, where a forlorn golfer decided to use the top of the Great Pyramid as a tee (page 288). Another striking scene from the desert was taken in Saudi Arabia (page 280). There a golfer named U.V. Stewart plays his approach from the desert sands onto a green of black-oiled sand at Rolling Hills Country Club in Dhahran. A description of this course appeared in the August 1953 issue of *USGA Journal*: "Picture, if you will, a sand bunker roughly 100 yards wide and 5,310 yards long, with occasional breaks where the hands of time dumped a few acres of boulders and hillocks. … Grass is only a memory, and there isn't a tree in the area. What looks like an easy course from the clubhouse is a nightmare, made no less harrowing by the 120-degree heat and the strong, dry winds." As these and other images show, golf can be found the world over in many forms and in surprising terrains.

Sandy and Fred Herd were among the earliest Scottish professionals to emigrate to America. Fred (right) wears the medal he was awarded for his victory in the 1898 U.S. Open.

(previous pages) A drive from the top of the Great Pyramids in the necropolis at Giza, just outside Cairo, Egypt.

(right) JoAnne Gunderson Carner, a member of the 1964 USA Curtis Cup Team, poses on the rocks at Royal Porthcawl Golf Club in Porthcawl, Wales.

(above) David "Auld Daw" Anderson (middle) serves up a glass of ginger beer to Old Tom Morris (right) from his cart on the 4th hole of the Old Course in St. Andrews, Scotland.

Ted Ray, the formidable English professional and winner of the 1920 U.S. Open.

Odette Lefebvre, a stylish European golfer, pictured in 1931.

The Stars and Stripes and the Union Jack fly during the opening ceremony of the 1967 Walker Cup Match

at Royal St. George's Golf Club in Sandwich, England.

(left) A tee sits precariously atop the cliffs at Victoria Golf Club on Vancouver Island in British Columbia, Canada.

(following pages) Old Tom Morris (left, in overcoat) looks on as Harry Vardon drives from the 1st tee of the Old Course at St. Andrews, circa 1900.

(above) A portrait of Old Tom Morris, the legendary professional and greenkeeper at St. Andrews, taken by noted American golf architect A.W. Tillinghast.

England's Cyril Tolley drives from the 10th tee at Royal Liverpool Golf Club in Hoylake, England, during his match against American Chick Evans, Jr. in 1921.

*Spectators gather to watch J. Lyndon Jones drive from the 1st tee during the 1931 British Amateur
at Royal North Devon Golf Club (Westward Ho!) in Devon, England.*

(previous pages) The gallery endures the rain during the 1937 Ryder Cup at Southport and Ainsdale Golf Club in Lancashire, England.

(left) Francis Ouimet blasts from a bunker on the 13th hole of the Old Course at St. Andrews during the 1923 Walker Cup.

(above) Teams representing the United States and Canada played one another at Toronto Golf Club in 1898.

(above) Bob Jones putts on the 11th green at Hoylake en route to victory in the 1930 British Open.

(following pages) The members of the 1936 USA Curtis Cup team.

Spectators get a better view during the 1921 British Open at St. Andrews.

(above) Four great British professionals: J.H. Taylor, Fred Herd, James Braid, and Harry Vardon.

(following pages) Golf on the links in Scotland during the late 19th century.

(right) "The Devil's Cauldron"—the 8th hole at Banff Springs Golf Course in Banff, Alberta, Canada.

*(following pages) The trophy presentation during the 1951 Walker Cup at
Royal Birkdale Golf Club in Southport, England.*

(below) 1931 British Open Champion Tommy Armour receives the Claret Jug from the Earl of Airlie.

Walter Hagen, playing in an exhibition match against British professional Archie Compston in 1928, attempts to extricate his ball

from a ditch on the 5th hole at Moor Park Golf Club in Rickmansworth, Hertfordshire, England.

PARTING SHOTS

IT'S NOT ABOUT THE BALL

Thomas L. Friedman

WHAT IS THE MYSTERY OF GOLF?

Whenever I ask myself that question I am always reminded of the joke that Woody Allen tells in the movie *Annie Hall*, which basically goes like this: "Doctor, Doctor, I have a terrible problem—my brother thinks he's a chicken." "That's crazy," says the doctor, "just tell him he's not a chicken." "I can't," the man says, "I need the eggs." That's me. That's why I keep coming back to this game of golf—bogeys, birdies, disappointments and thrills—because I need the eggs. And what are those? What are those irrational, intangible, often indescribable, things about this game that constantly bring us back for more?

Every golfer will have his or her own list. But what they all have in common is this: It's not about the ball. Oh, you golfers know what I mean. How many times have you heard a non-golfer scoff at you and say, "Golf! What a silly game—four hours, four people, chasing around a little white ball." Or, as President Ulysses S. Grant reportedly observed upon first encountering the game—as recounted in the introduction to the book *Presidential Lies: The Illustrated History of White House Golf* by Shepherd Campbell and Peter Landau—"That does look like very good exercise, but what is the little ball for?" What these non-golfers don't get is this:

It's not about the ball. It's about everything else.

(previous pages) English professional Archie Compston drives from the 9th tee during the 1929 Ryder Cup at Moortown Golf Club in Leeds, England.

(left) Pre-dawn putting practice.

I know this to be true, because when I think back on my golf life as a young boy growing up in Minnesota, what I remember most warmly today aren't my scores or any particular shots—although those were very important and I do indeed remember many. What I remember *most*, what brings me a certain inner glow, are the people. I remember my dad following me around at every high school golf match. I remember our club—the locker room, the caddie shack, the men's grill, the weekend brunches and the Sunday night bingo. I remember special bonds as much as special birdies, and lessons about the real world, as much as lessons about the ideal swing plane. And I remember the arc of different golf shots framed against the landscapes and horizons of my youth, something that is mirrored in its purest form in the magnificent pictures collected in this book.

I would like to talk a little about each of these intangibles. Let me start with the most primordial aspect of the game, one that dates back thousands of years to our days as hunter-gatherers, and that is we are social beings, and we are most happy when we are located and anchored in a family, in a community, in a regular foursome, in a club. There is no other sport that builds the unique bonds between father and son, parent and child, or friend and friend, the way golf does, because there is no other sport that involves a four-hour walk in the woods, with competition and conversation so intimately intertwined. Golf is a good walk enhanced—not spoiled.

My golf friendships are like no others. My steady fellow competitor for more than a decade, Joel Finkelstein, likes to say that he would rather shoot 85 with his regular friends than 75 with three strangers. It really is true. If I shoot a record round on vacation or out of town, or, God forbid, were to have a hole-in-one—and my regular partners were not there to pay to watch—well, it would be like a tree falling in the forest. Who would know about it? And who would care? It would be as if it never happened.

How many other sports have regular father and son or daughter tournaments each year at clubs around the country? It is a tribal ritual unique to golf. Like so many, I learned the game starting at age five, playing with my father at our club outside Minneapolis, using a sawed-off driver. I can still see that club in my mind's eye. It was probably about 18 inches long. The clubhead was an old wood and the grip was made of black electrician's tape, wound around the mini-steel shaft. I don't remember many shots with it, but I remember the first time I made a bogey on the 18th hole at our home club: Dogleg left. Three shots to get on. Two putts. Bang. Hooked for life.

Every summer my dad and I had the same routine: He would come home from work around 5:30 p.m., we would rush through dinner and then get in six or seven holes before the sun went down. It was during those summer evenings with my dad that I first learned to appreciate the intellectual side of golf, even though I never could have articulated it at the time. Golf has a very unique, but underrated, intellectual dimension and it's all about how the game's best golf courses force you to combine geometry and geography. They force you to factor in the wind speed, the angle of the lie and then the precise geometry of the shot needed to carry the trees, water, hillock or bunker and nestle near the flag. The most satisfying thing about golf is not only defining the exact geometry equation in your head, but then physically pulling off the shot that solves that equation on the course. The most precious and satisfying seconds in golf are watching a ball that you have struck perfectly match the geography, soar at just the right trajectory, bounce at just the right angle and finish right by the hole—if not in it! It is not like smashing a homerun in baseball or an overhead in tennis. That's just about muscle. And it's not like throwing a long-bomb in football. That requires someone else's skill as well to catch it. It is a unique combination of mind, muscle and matter that is unparalleled in sport.

Scott Simon, the NPR News Host, put this best when he told the magazine *T&L Golf* (January–February 2001) what he enjoyed most about the game: "Even for just a chip or a pitch," said Simon, "there is something so ineffably satisfying about seeing the ball soar in a harmonious arc that is headed toward something. It's almost like solving a math problem. Same kind of a resonance and satisfaction. Hitting a golf ball at that level enables you to understand a very small part of the world—like tying a knot."

My dad and I repeated our evening golf ritual for twelve summers—from when I was six until I was eighteen. Until we couldn't anymore. My dad died of a heart attack on the 15th green at Rolling Greens Country Club on June 6, 1973. He lied three.

Given our history of golf together, I was always sort of happy that he didn't die at his gray desk, or in some lonely, sterile hospital ward attended by nurses, but that he died under a summer sun, playing the game he loved, with the friends he adored. My only regret was that he never got to finish the hole.

I so wished he would have pared in.

LIKE SO MANY OTHERS, I didn't just learn about golf on the golf course. I first learned about the birdies and the bees—and a whole lot more—as a caddie. Indeed, looking back now I realize I learned about so many things, for the first time, on the golf course. I remember walking down the fairway as a very young man and my dad talking about a childhood friend of his who had been arrested a long time ago. I think it was in the time of Prohibition, when Minneapolis had its own little Mafias. I asked him what this acquaintance of his had done and my dad tried to break it to me gently, saying: "He was shopping in a store before it opened." It was the best euphemism for armed robbery I've ever heard. Never forgot it. My dad had a friend he played with regularly and one day he dropped out of our club, moved to Chicago and got divorced at the same time. He was a funny, nice man, with coke-bottle glasses, who was a regular in my

Naree Song Wongluekiet during the 2002 Women's World Amateur Team Championship in Kuala Lumpur, Malaysia.

father's foursome. When I asked my dad what happened to this man, he explained that he had gone "bankrupt." I was too young to understand what bankruptcy was, but I was old enough to understand its consequences: bankruptcy meant that all of a sudden you couldn't play golf any more. You were DQ'd. You were Out of Bounds and out of balls. It was really a shock to me, which is again, why I remembered it forty years later. Life for a middle-class kid in Minneapolis in those days was pretty placid. I had no idea that people went bankrupt and that golf, not to mention life, could be suddenly aborted, just like that.

Certainly one of my most pleasurable life tutorials came from caddieing at age 16, for Juan (Chi Chi) Rodriguez in the 1970 U.S. Open at Hazeltine National Golf Club in Chaska, Minnesota, a few miles from where I grew up. Yes, you read that correctly. Believe it or not, there was an age before celebrity caddies, swing coaches and managerial entourages, an age before everything was professionalized, commercialized, commoditized and advertised, an age when local caddies like me got to carry the bags of the world's best golfers in the world's most important golf championship. It was an age when the USGA insisted that professionals not be allowed to use professional caddies at the Open, because it might give them an advantage over the amateurs. So, instead, the host club—in this case, Hazeltine—enlisted all the area clubs to contribute their best caddies for the event. A few weeks before the championship, we, the lucky local caddies nominated for the Open, were gathered in the dining room at Hazeltine. There, the names of all the golfers had been put into a big glass bowl. The names Jack Nicklaus and Arnold Palmer, Sam Snead and Gary Player were in there with Bunky Henry and Dudley Wysong. We each walked up and pulled a name out of the bowl to see whose bag we would tote. I pulled Chi Chi.

The first time Chi Chi and I met he said to me, "Tom, if I win this championship I am going to put you through college." Then he paused for a moment and said, "I hope you're a senior in college."

One day Chi Chi and I were standing on the practice tee, and Chi Chi was hitting shots and providing a running commentary. There was a small crowd watching from behind the ropes.

"You know, I used to be a teacher," Chi Chi told the fans, as he whacked balls. "But I gave that up. You know why? You know why? I had this woman, she was a slicer, and I turned her into a hooker, and after that I gave up teaching."

Well, I was all of 16 at the time and, I confess, I did not know what a hooker was and why all these adults around me were laughing. My dad had to explain it to me. Chi Chi did quite well at Hazeltine. In fact, he was in second place after the first day, shooting a 73. We ended up coming in 27th place, which was one of his better finishes ever in the Open. He paid me $175 dollars and gave me all the balls and gloves in his bag. He was a real gentleman. I am so grateful to have had the chance to get to know him a little.

About 20 years after the Open, after I had become a foreign correspondent for *The New York Times*, won two Pulitzer Prizes and written a best-selling book, some close family friends of ours from Minneapolis ran into Chi Chi at the Innisbrook Resort in Palm Harbor, Florida. They struck up a conversation, told him that they had followed him at Hazeltine in 1970 and asked if he remembered who caddied for him there. Chi Chi thought for a moment and, to my friends' surprise, said, "Tommy." My friends then said to Chi Chi—with great overstatement—"Do you know that Tommy's more famous than you are today?" Chi Chi thought about that for a second and said—with perfect understatement: "Not in Puerto Rico."

There was something Chi Chi had in common with my dad and his fellow competitors that always appealed to me. He had a sense of the "undertow," a sense that no matter how good things seemed, life was a fragile thing and at any moment it could all disappear. Because both Chi Chi and my father had grown up poor, they knew that no matter how good you were playing, no matter how much you were up in the Nassau, a triple bogey could grab you at anytime. It wasn't ever expressed directly, but always just in little asides or statements Chi Chi or my dad made while strolling down the fairway.

When my dad and I would drive out to our club we always passed this intersection, and my dad often reminded me that during the depression there was some kind of labor camp there where he had worked. At the end of each day, he recalled, he would buy a loaf of bread for his meal for a couple of pennies. "I can still feel that bread getting caught in my throat," he would tell me. In fact, he told me so many times, I used to tease him as we would drive by, "I can still feel that bread getting caught in my throat …"

Chi Chi too definitely knew there were 18 holes in life and that they all weren't pars and birdies. In particular, I remember him pointing out another pro and whispering to me that he had just overheard that guy complaining about the food in the locker room—and what an ungrateful jerk he was. Among Chi Chi's standard lines was to point to a row of portable potties over in the rough and describe them as "Puerto Rican condominiums," or to confide that "I was such a little kid I got my start in golf as a ball marker." Alas, self-deprecation is a lost art today among professional athletes.

Whenever I've had a chance to speak to good young amateur golfers, I've tried to encourage them not to become one of those athletes who is totally oblivious to current events, never reads anything but the sports section and who thinks that the country club life *is* life. This game has given us all a lot, and we honor it not only by playing by its rules. We honor it by, as golfers, taking responsibility for the communities and the world beyond the 18th tee. In a flat world, if you don't visit a bad neighborhood, eventually it will visit you.

Tom Watson is not only passionate about golf, but also world affairs. We got to know each

The 5th green at Pumpkin Ridge Golf Club in North Plains, Oregon during the 2003 U.S. Women's Open.

other at a charity event and have since become email pen pals—me chatting about golf and him about world affairs. In the summer of 2006, I was in Damascus, Syria, covering the Israel-Hezbollah war, and I noted in the local paper that Tom had made the cut in the British Open. So I emailed him my congratulations and gave him an update on the news from Syria. Tom's caddie, Neil Oxman, who replaced the late Bruce Edwards, is also a friend. Neil is actually a renowned Democratic political consultant who caddies for Tom in non-election years. The next day in Damascus I got this email from Neil. It read: "So I'm at Hoylake caddieing for Watson on Saturday at the Open. Watson starts out with a double, then birdies three and four, and as we're walking off the fifth tee, he starts gabbing about the fact that he's exchanging emails with you while you're in Damascus. I'm just trying to figure out the yardage for the second shot and he's preoccupied with the Middle East." Then Neil added, and this was my favorite part, "but he still birdied the hole!"

WHICH LEADS TO MY NEXT POINT: Golf won't necessarily build character, but it will always reveal character. That's why I have always been so attracted to the idea that golf, more than any other sport, is like life and therefore it reveals more about an individual's character in a short time than any other sport. The cliché is true: Play a round of golf with someone and you will learn everything you need to know about them in four hours.

Why? Let's start with some statistics. I once read that Dave Pelz, the famous putting guru, discovered that the best players in the world miss half their six-foot putt attempts and more than three-quarters of their 10-foot putt attempts. According to one National Golf Foundation study I read about in *Pebble Beach* magazine in the summer of 2001, out of the 26 million golfers in America, only 22 percent break 90 regularly and only 6 percent of men and 1 percent of women break 80 regularly. The average score for men is 97 and for women 114. Randy Johnson, the three-time Cy Young Award-winning pitcher, and an avid golfer, was once asked to describe the most annoying thing about golf, as compared to baseball. "It's the inability to repeat," he told *Golf Digest* in October 2001. "You play one hole great, then go to the next tee box, and it's gone. What did I do wrong? Why?"

"Doesn't that happen in pitching?" he was asked.

"To an extent, yes. If I start a game without my best stuff, then I have to really pitch more and try to get by without overpowering batters. But golf is more complicated. Too many more facets."

What Johnson and the statisticians are telling us is something every golfer knows: Golf is a game that cannot be mastered. It involves a lot of unnatural motions that you initiate yourself and, worse, it is played on a deliberately uneven surface that produces good and bad breaks on every hole. Sure football has its crazy bounces, but it is played on a perfectly flat surface that is meant to minimize the number of wild bounces and produce ones that are as predictable as possible. The same with tennis, bowling, and baseball. In tennis you even get a do-over if your serve caroms wildly off the net, but stays in bounds. Not in golf. In golf you don't get a do-over because your ball, struck perfectly, heading right for the hole, hits the flagstick and caroms 90 feet away. Golf has no standardized playing fields, it is designed for unpredictable bounces. In fact, golf celebrates the unpredictable and even enshrines it in the rules of the game.

One of the first items in the USGA's Rules of Golf is the term "The rub of the green." The rub of the green refers to the fact that you may drive your ball 300 yards straight down the middle of the fairway and then find that it has landed in a divot. Too bad, you must play it out of there—that's just the rub of the green. As in golf, so in life, there are no do-overs. You have to play it where it lies.

It is precisely because golf is a game that can never be mastered in any lasting way, and is inherently full of crazy bounces, that makes it such a revealing test of character—both your own and that of the people you are playing with. It is a cliché but it's true: spend four hours with someone playing 18 holes and you will learn just about everything you need to know about them, by watching how they treat their caddie, how they treat their fellow competitors, whether they whine and blame others for their failures, or take things in stride, whether they are patient or impatient, and whether they play by the rules or prefer to cheat. The guy who takes responsibility for a bad shot in golf will do so in life. Jack Welch, the legendary former chairman of GE, is a talented golfer and I once asked him about how he used golf to take the measure of others: "I think you can certainly detect a flawed character on the golf course," Welch remarked. "Because you are out with people for four hours, it gives you a chance to really be with them in all sorts of situations—in bunkers, after the round, when they are up, when they are down, to see whether they are good winners or bad winners. To see whether they mark their ball properly? Do they throw clubs? Do they shave strokes? There are a whole series of tell-tale signs and they all come out on the golf course over four hours."

I played golf with President Clinton, right at the end of his presidency. It was post-Monica, post-impeachment, post-everything. I had an assignment from *Golf Digest* to interview Clinton about his years as the most golfing president. We played at the Army-Navy Club in Virginia. One of the first questions I asked him was whether he thought there were any parallels between golf and life. His answer intrigued me—not just because of what it revealed about golf, but because of what it revealed about his whole turbulent tenure.

"Golf is like life in a lot of ways," Clinton said to me. "The most important competition is the one against yourself. All the biggest wounds are self-inflicted. And you get a lot of breaks you don't deserve—both ways. So it's important not to get too upset when you're having a bad day."

There is one specific aspect of character that I think golf always reveals, although it isn't spoken about much—and that is a willingness to work at something. As in golf, so in life, you can't buy a game. You have to work at it, you have to build a solid foundation. Golf is simply not a game that you can just pick up a club and be good at right away. Even if you are a natural athlete or a natural golfer, you have to constantly practice and take lessons. The only way you can even hope to master this game that can't be mastered is with good fundamentals. Gary Player has a saying that always struck home with me: "The more I practice, the luckier I get." I am a big believer that Tiger Woods is the best golfer and Michael Jordan is the best basketball player, not because they have more natural talent than everyone else, but because they work harder and practice more than everyone else, on top of their natural talent. No one can master this game. It comes and goes— even for the best of them—which is why one of my favorite golf quotes is the one attributed to a teaching pro, who, when asked by a student why he gave lessons, answered: "I give lessons to people like you so I can make money to take lessons myself."

THE FACT THAT GOLF CANNOT BE MASTERED and is inherently full of crazy bounces is also what makes the Rules of Golf so important. Just as the rule of law is the bedrock of our society, upon which all good things rest, so the Rules of Golf are the bedrock on which all the fun of golf rests.

Why? Because the natural human tendency is to want to play the game in a way that will allow you to consistently master it, and to remove all the unpredictable bounces and lies. The rules, however, are designed to protect the game's essential character by protecting it from those manufacturers or hackers who want to excessively compensate for its difficulties and unpredictability.

We need to remember that by protecting the game's essential character this way, the Rules of Golf are also protecting the essential thrill of the game that keeps us coming back. Because the thrill of golf, one of the eggs that keeps us coming back time after time, are those rare times when, for one hole, one side, even one round, we momentarily master the game, triumph over all its crazy bounces and score our career low—*within the rules of the game*. That is, within a common standard that any golfer anywhere would recognize and appreciate.

Without those rules, maintained by the USGA, without that common standard, our game would never be fun, because we would never be able to compare ourselves to ourselves or to others. The pictures in this book would have no meaning. There would never be a sense of triumph. Think about it: If my rules were that you could kick the ball out of all bad lies, to overcome golf's essential unpredictability, and your rules were that you could use an illegal driver that launches the ball so far that no bunker would ever be in the way, and thereby allow you to master a game that could never be mastered, there would be no feeling of: "I did it! I beat this hole. I beat this course!

I beat the standard." It is precisely the Rules of Golf that allow us to brag, "Let me tell you about my great round. I want to describe every shot."

Because golf, like life, cannot be mastered and is full of crazy bounces the key to getting through both is the same: You have to understand that there are 18 holes and you can't let the inevitable bad shots or bad bounces ruin your journey. You never know what's waiting for you at the next tee or on the next green, so press on.

I learned that from the moment I started playing. For my 10th birthday my dad ordered me my very own set of golf clubs from the Northwestern Golf Company, based at the time, I believe, in Chicago. Up to then, I had been playing with a mixed set of hand-me-downs. Well, I waited every day for that delivery truck to show up with my junior clubs. It was one of those starter sets —driver, three wood, putter, 3, 5, 7, and 9 irons, plus a bag. I don't think there was a wedge.

One day that delivery truck rolled up at our house, and it dropped off a tall cardboard box. I ripped it open and inside were my shiny new golf clubs. My own sticks! I pulled them out one by one, removed the plastic covers, wrapped my fingers around those blue Northwestern grips, set up in my stance and immediately discovered that something was terribly, terribly wrong: The clubs were all left-handed.

I, on the other hand, was all right-handed.

You cannot imagine the crushing disappointment I felt having to rewrap those clubs, put them back in the box and send them back to the Northwestern Golf Company in Chicago. It would be weeks more before my right-handed set would come. So from day one I learned one of golf's most important lessons—you have to be patient and hang in there.

I am sure the single piece of advice I have given most often to young journalists is to be patient. If things are not going just right for you in your job right now, don't just pick up or walk out. Tough it out for a while. Make the turn. The back nine could be totally different. The important thing is not what you score on one hole. It's the score you turn in at the end of the round. Remember, in golf and life, there are 18 holes.

What comes after that, well, who knows. The legendary sports writer Jim Murray once told the following story: "I'm gambling that when we get into the next life, Saint Peter will look at us and ask, 'Golfer?' And when we nod, he will step aside and say, 'Go right in, you've suffered enough.' One warning [though], if you go in and the first thing you see is a par 3 surrounded by water, it ain't heaven."

THOMAS L. FRIEDMAN is the Foreign Affairs columnist for *The New York Times*, author of *The World Is Flat*, a contributing editor to *Golf Digest* and a long-time member of the USGA.

American Chris Nallen plays his approach to the 18th green during the 2003 Walker Cup at Ganton Golf Club in North Yorkshire, England.

ILLUSTRATIONS CREDITS

All photos courtesy of the USGA Archives; Photo credit and/or copyright unknown unless otherwise specified:

2–3, John Mummert/USGA; 4, J.D. Cuban/USGA; 20–21, John Mummert/USGA; 23, John Mummert/USGA; 24–25, Robert Walker/USGA; 26–27, J.D. Cuban/USGA; 33, Robert Walker/USGA; 34–35, Photograph by George S. Pietzcker; 36, J.D. Cuban/USGA; 37, Steven Gibbons/USGA; 39, John Mummert/USGA; 41, John Mummert/USGA; 42, J.D. Cuban/USGA; 43, Steven Gibbons/USGA; 44-45, L.C. Lambrecht/USGA; 46, John Mummert/USGA; 47, John Mummert/USGA; 48, John Mummert/USGA; 49, John Mummert/USGA; 52, John Mummert/USGA; 53, John Mummert/USGA; 54, Robert Walker/USGA; 55, John Mummert/USGA; 56–57, AP/Wide World Photos; 58, AP/Wide World Photos; 59, John Mummert/USGA; 63, John Mummert/USGA; 64–65, John Mummert/USGA; 69, L.C. Lambrecht/USGA; 70–71, L.C. Lambrecht/USGA; 73, James Drake/Sports Illustrated; 76–77, Photograph by H.A. Strohmeyer; 78–79, Phil Arnold/USGA; 80, Photograph by George S. Pietzcker; 84–85, John Mummert/USGA; 87, John Mummert/USGA; 89, John Mummert/USGA; 90, Steven Gibbons/USGA; 91, John Mummert/USGA; 92–93, L.C. Lambrecht/USGA; 94, John Mummert/USGA; 95, John Mummert/USGA; 101, John Mummert/USGA; 98–99, Photograph by H.A. Strohmeyer; 102, John Mummert/USGA; 103, John Mummert/USGA (Bottom Right); 104–105, John Mummert/USGA; 106–107, John Mummert/USGA; 108, John Mummert/USGA; 113, John Mummert/USGA; 116, John Mummert/USGA; 117, John Mummert/USGA; 118, John Mummert/USGA; 119, John Mummert/USGA; 120–121, Phil Arnold/USGA; 122, Photograph by George S. Pietzcker; 124–125, Phil Arnold/USGA; 126, Steven Gibbons/USGA; 127, Steven Gibbons/USGA; 128, John Mummert/USGA; 129, John Mummert/USGA; 130–131, John Mummert/USGA; 132, John Mummert/USGA; 133, John Mummert/USGA; 134, AP/Wide World Photos; 136–137, John Mummert/USGA; 138, John Mummert/USGA; 139, John Mummert/USGA; 142, AP/Wide World Photos; 143, AP/Wide World Photos; 144–145, Russell Kirk/USGA; 146, J.D. Cuban/USGA; 147, John Mummert/USGA; 148, John Mummert/USGA; 149, John Mummert/USGA; 150–151, John Mummert/USGA; 152, John Mummert/USGA; 153, John Mummert/USGA; 154, Robert Walker/USGA; 155, John Mummert/USGA; 156–157, L.C. Lambrecht/USGA; 158–159, John Mummert/USGA; 165, John Mummert/USGA; 168, John Mummert/USGA; 169, Robert Walker/USGA; 171, Joann Dost/USGA; 172–173, Phil Arnold/USGA; 174, AP/Wide World Photos; 175, AP/Wide World Photos; 178, John Mummert/USGA; 179, John Mummert/USGA; 180–181, John Mummert/USGA; 186, John Mummert/USGA; 187, Robert Walker/USGA; 188–89, John Mummert/USGA; 190, John Mummert/USGA; 191, John Mummert/USGA; 195, John Mummert/USGA; 196, John Mummert/USGA; 197, John Mummert/USGA; 198–199, L.C. Lambrecht/USGA; 200, AP/Wide World Photos; 204, John Mummert/USGA; 205, John Mummert/USGA; 206-207, Robert Walker/USGA; 214, John Mummert/USGA; 215, John Mummert/USGA; 216–217, L.C. Lambrecht/USGA; 218, John Mummert/USGA; 221, Larry Petrillio/USGA (left); 221, USGA Archives/USGA (far right); 222, John Mummert/USGA; 223, Richard Dole/USGA; 224-225, John Mummert/USGA; 226–227, John Mummert/USGA; 230, John Mummert/USGA; 235, John Mummert/USGA; 238, John Mummert/USGA; 239, Warren Morgan/USGA; 240-241, John Mummert/USGA; 242, John Mummert/USGA; 243, John Mummert/USGA; 244-245, John Mummert/USGA; 248–249, John Mummert/USGA; 250, John Mummert/USGA; 251, J.D. Cuban/USGA; 252–253, John Mummert/USGA; 254, John Mummert/USGA; 255, Sam Greenwood/USGA; 260–261, John Mummert/USGA; 262, John Mummert/USGA; 263, John Mummert/USGA; 264–265, John Mummert/USGA; 266, John Mummert/USGA; 267, John Mummert/USGA; 268–269, John Mummert/USGA; 272, Robert Walker/USGA; 273, John Mummert/USGA; 274, John Mummert/USGA; 275, John Mummert/USGA; 276–277, Farewell Mills Gatsch LLC/USGA ; 280–281, Photograph by T.F. Walters; 292, Photograph by George S; Pietzcker; 297, Photograph by A.W. Tillinghast; 322, John Mummert/USGA; 326-327, John Mummert/USGA; 330-331, John Mummert/USGA; 336–337, John Mummert/USGA; 346–347, John Mummert/USGA.

ACKNOWLEDGMENTS

Despite what the title page may say, few books—and especially this one—represent the contributions of a sole individual. The entire USGA Communications Department played a positive role in making this book happen. Many of the members of the department lent a direct hand; some picked up the slack so others could free enough time to make crucial contributions.

This blanket praise, however, shortchanges some folks who require individual mention. Special thanks are extended to these members (past and present) of the USGA staff: Rand Jerris, John Mummert, Ellie Kaiser, Jaime Mikle, Doug Stark, Nancy Stulack, Cheryl Badini, Corinne Felice, Belinda Berman, David Shefter, Beth Murrison, Rhonda Glenn, Pete Kowalski, Becky Sandquist, Kim Barney, Dick Rugge, Kimberly Erusha, and Patty Moran, who patiently and meticulously dug out piles of documents used in the essays without ever losing her cheer.

This project simply could not have happened without the support of Fiona Dolan and all who work for the USGA Members Program. Likewise, Mary Lopuszynski who handles all USGA merchandising with consummate skill lent her early and steadfast blessing.

Tom Friedman of *The New York Times* graciously accepted our proposal to take time away from his writing of Pulitzer-Prize winning columns and best-selling books to write his essay for this book. I wish to thank him for his thoughtfulness, friendship and kindness to me and our Association.

We wish to say thank you to the National Geographic Society for being the best publisher possible in this venture, our second book with them. We especially need to cite the consistent hard work of Ellen Beal, who spearheaded the project for NGS, as well as acknowledge Dana Chivvis, Cinda Rose, Kevin Mulroy, and Chris Liedel of NGS. We also want to thank NGS for securing the assistance of two fellow New Jersey residents, Davi Cohen and John Paine. Davi helped us select photographs with skill and good cheer. John, meanwhile, labored to edit and improve our written words.

Last but not least, appreciation must be extended to the members of the USGA Executive Committee, all committee volunteers, and USGA Executive Director David Fay for providing the tools and support necessary for such a long-term undertaking as this one.

DEDICATION

Two individuals — Bob Sommers and Mark Mulvoy— must share the credit here. That's okay because they know and like each other. I can attest because the three of us shared a delightful, long lunch together one day in March in Florida two years ago. I'm still smiling every time I think about their banter back-and-forth across the table …

Bob skillfully served the USGA from 1966–1991 in a number of capacities, most notably as editor of *Golf Journal*. He made the fateful decision to hire me in 1991. I suspect the Association forced him to retire shortly thereafter as just retribution. For giving me that chance and much else he has taught me since that time, I am eternally grateful.

Mark, meanwhile, is a former volunteer on our USGA Communications Committee. He's best known as the long-time managing editor of *Sports Illustrated*. He possesses a lively, keen intellect with an incredible eye for the power of the photographic image. His lessons have, thankfully, never ceased since I've become fortunate to know him. He has changed every philosophy about communications that I possess — and always for the better.

Both rank among the best of mentors. But they are even greater gentlemen. Until our next lunch together, I can only offer this dedication as an indication of my deepest appreciation.

USGA TIMELINE 1894–2006

1894

- In September, William G. Lawrence wins a "national amateur championship" at Newport Golf Club, Newport, RI. In October, Laurence B. Stoddart wins a "national amateur championship" at The St. Andrew's Golf Club in Yonkers, NY.
- Charles B. Macdonald, runner-up in both the Newport Golf Club and The St. Andrew's Golf Club events, calls for the formation of a governing body to run a universally recognized national championship.
- The Amateur Golf Association of the United States — soon to be called the United States Golf Association — is formed. Charter members are Newport Golf Club, Shinnecock Hills Golf Club, The Country Club (in Brookline, MA), The St. Andrew's Golf Club, and Chicago Golf Club.

1895

- Charles B. Macdonald wins the first official U.S. Amateur Championship at Newport Golf Club. The first U.S. Open is held the next day at the same club. Horace Rawlins wins the $150 first prize in a field of eleven.
- Mrs. Charles S. Brown (Lucy Barnes) wins the first U.S. Women's Amateur Championship at Meadow Brook Club in Hempstead, NY.

1896

- James Foulis wins the second official U.S. Open, held at Shinnecock Hills Golf Club.
- John Shippen, an African-American professional, and Oscar Bunn, a Shinnecock Indian, compete in the U.S. Open despite a threatened boycott by the other contestants. Shippen finishes fifth.

1897

- Joe Lloyd is victorious in the third U.S. Open, held at Chicago Golf Club.
- H.J. Whigham wins his second U.S. Amateur.

1898

- Beatrix Hoyt wins her third consecutive U.S. Women's Amateur at Ardsley Club in Ardsley-on-Hudson, NY. Two years later, she retires at the age of 20.
- Coburn Haskell and Bertram Work design and patent a wound-rubber golf ball, which flies farther than the gutta-percha ball.
- The U.S. Open expands to 72 holes from 36 and is held for the first time at a separate course from the Amateur.

1900

- British star Harry Vardon shows Americans how to play the game. In the country for an exhibition tour, he wins the U.S. Open over fellow Englishman J.H. Taylor. Vardon becomes the first sports figure to endorse a sporting goods product, using a Spalding Vardon Flyer ball throughout the tour.
- Americans Charles Sands and Margaret Abbott win gold medals in golf in the Olympic Games in Paris.
- Walter Travis, who took up golf in 1896 at age 35, wins the U.S. Amateur.

1901

- Walter Travis wins his second consecutive U.S. Amateur and publishes an instructional book entitled *Practical Golf*. He's the first golfer to win a major championship playing a Haskell wound-rubber ball.
- Willie Anderson ties Alex Smith with a record-high 331 in the U.S. Open and takes the play-off with an 85.

1902

- Willie Anderson wins the Western Open with a 299 total, the first time 300 is broken for 72 holes in an American event.

1903

- Walter Travis, known as "The Old Man," wins his third U.S. Amateur at the age of 41.
- Willie Anderson sets U.S. Open records with a 72 in the final round and a 303 total.

1905

- Twenty-five-year-old Willie Anderson wins his third consecutive U.S. Open and fourth in five years. It is also his last Open victory; he dies in 1910.

1906

- Three-time runner-up Alex Smith finally wins the U.S. Open, becoming the first to break 300 for the 72-hole championship. His brother, Willie, is second.

1907

- Margaret Curtis beats her sister Harriot in an all-in-the-family final of the U.S. Women's Amateur.

1908

- Jerry Travers wins his second consecutive U.S. Amateur.

1909

- Robert Gardner becomes the youngest U.S. Amateur champion at age 19.
- The USGA rules that caddies, caddiemasters and greenkeepers past the age of 16 are professionals. The age would be raised to 18 in 1930, 21 in 1945, until the ruling is rescinded in 1963.

1910

- The R&A bans the center-shafted putter, while the USGA keeps it legal, marking the first time that the USGA diverges from an R&A equipment ruling.
- Alex Smith wins his second U.S. Open by beating his other brother, Macdonald.

1911

- Johnny McDermott signals the end of dominance by Scottish-born professionals in early American golf by becoming the first native to win the U.S. Open. At 19, he's also the youngest winner ever.
- Englishman Harold Hilton is the first player to win the British and U.S. Amateur in the same year.

- The USGA increased yardage for determining par:

    Three — up to 225 yards
    Four — 225 to 425 yards
    Five — 426 to 600 yards
    Six — more than 600 yards

1912

- The USGA introduces a handicap limit of six on entrants for the U.S. Amateur.

1913

- Twenty-year-old American amateur Francis Ouimet stages the game's biggest upset, beating English stars Harry Vardon and Ted Ray in a playoff to win the U.S. Open at The Country Club in Brookline, MA. The resultant headlines spark a surge of interest in the game in America.
- Jerry Travers wins his fourth U.S. Amateur.

1914

- Walter Hagen, a stylish 21-year-old professional, wins the first of his two U.S. Open titles, leading after every round.
- Francis Ouimet becomes the first with career U.S. Open and Amateur titles, beating Jerry Travers in the final of the U.S. Amateur.

1915

- Jerry Travers adds the U.S. Open to his four U.S. Amateur championships and then retires at 28.

1916

- The amateur run on the U.S. Open continues. Chick Evans is the third amateur to win in four years, shooting a record 286. He is also the first to capture the U.S. Open and Amateur titles in the same year.
- Fourteen-year-old phenom and future champion Bob Jones makes his U.S. Amateur debut, reaching the quarterfinals at Merion Cricket Club in Ardmore, PA.

1917

- USGA championships (U.S. Open, U.S. Amateur, U.S. Women's Amateur) and the PGA Championship are suspended in 1917 and 1918 because of World War I.

- Par yardage is again changed:

    Three — up to 250 yards
    Four — 251 to 445 yards
    Five — 446 to 600 yards
    Six — more than 600 yards

1918

- The USGA sponsors tournaments and exhibitions throughout the country to raise money for the war effort. Among the professional and amateur golfers who participate are the Dixie Kids—featuring Atlanta teenagers Perry Adair, Watts Gunn, Bob Jones and Alexa Stirling—who raise $150,000 for the Red Cross.

1920

- Harry Vardon, 50, competing in his third U.S. Open, plays the last seven holes in even fives to finish second, one stroke behind his English countryman, 43-year-old Ted Ray. Ray becomes the oldest man to win the Open (a record that will stand until 1963).
- Alexa Stirling wins her third consecutive Women's Amateur (1916, 1919, 1920—the championship wasn't held in 1917 and 1918).
- The USGA creates the Green Section for turfgrass research.
- The USGA and R&A agree to a standard ball —1.62 inches in diameter and 1.62 ounces.

1921

- Jim Barnes romps to a nine-stroke win in the U.S. Open and President Warren Harding, a USGA Executive Committee member, presents the trophy at Columbia Country Club near Washington, DC.

1922

- A Cinderella story: 20-year-old Gene Sarazen, a sixth-grade dropout from a working-class family, wins the U.S. Open and PGA Championships.
- An admission fee ($1) is charged for the first time at the U.S. Open.
- Intended for all interested countries, the first Walker Cup Match between amateurs from the United States and Great Britain (the only taker) is held at National Golf Links of America in Southampton, NY. The U.S. wins.
- Public-course golfers receive their own competition — the USGA's Amateur Public Links Championship.

- Glenna Collett Vare wins her first of six U.S. Women's Amateur titles.

1923

- After several near-misses in the U.S. Open and U.S. Amateur, Bob Jones, 21, claims his first major title by beating Bobby Cruickshank in a playoff for the U.S. Open.

1924

- Steel-shafted clubs are permitted in the United States by the USGA as of April 11; the R&A continues to ban their use in Great Britain until 1929.
- Bob Jones wins the first of his five U.S. Amateur titles, at Merion Cricket Club.
- The USGA introduces sectional qualifying rounds for the U.S. Open.

1925

- Willie Macfarlane shoots a record 67 in the second round of the U.S. Open and goes on to defeat Bob Jones in a playoff.
- The Havemeyer Trophy, which is presented to the U.S. Amateur champion, is destroyed in a fire at Bob Jones' home club, East Lake, in Atlanta.

1926

- Bob Jones is the first to win the U.S. and British Opens in the same year.

1928

- Bob Jones and Glenna Collett Vare continue to dominate amateur golf. Jones wins the U.S. Amateur final by a 10-and-9 margin. Collett Vare claims the Women's Amateur, 13 and 12.

1929

- The U.S. Amateur goes to the West Coast for the first time, at Pebble Beach Golf Links. Bob Jones is the victim of a first-round upset, while Minnesota's Harrison "Jimmy" Johnston is crowned the champion.

1930

- Bob Jones wins the Grand Slam—the U.S. Open, U.S. Amateur, British Open and British Amateur—then retires at age 28.
- Glenna Collett Vare wins her third consecutive U.S. Women's Amateur.

1931

- The USGA mandates use of a larger and lighter ball (1.68 inches and 1.55 ounces). This so-called "balloon ball" is very unpopular, and after only one year the USGA increases the allowed weight to 1.62 ounces, keeping the size at 1.68 inches. Meanwhile, the R&A stays with the 1.62-inch, 1.62-ounce ball.
- The concave-faced wedge is banned, but Gene Sarazen perfects his design of the sand wedge with a wide flange, which will remain legal.
- Billy Burke is the first to win a U.S. Open using steel shafts. It takes him seventy-two extra holes (two thirty-six-hole playoffs) to beat George Von Elm.

1932

- Gene Sarazen wins the U.S. Open and British Open, with record scores of 286 and 283, respectively. He finishes the U.S. Open with a record 66.
- The first Curtis Cup Match, between women amateurs of the U.S. and Great Britain, is won by the United States, 5-1/2 to 3-1/2.

1933

- Johnny Goodman becomes the fifth and last amateur to win the U.S. Open.

1934

- Lawson Little wins the U.S. Amateur and British Amateur, the "Little Slam," a feat he will repeat in 1935.
- Virginia Van Wie wins the U.S. Women's Amateur for the third consecutive year.
- Joseph C. Dey Jr., is appointed Executive Secretary of the USGA. He will hold the post for 34 years.

1935

- Glenna Collett Vare wins her sixth U.S. Women's Amateur.

1936

- Lawson Little turns professional instead of going for a third consecutive U.S. Amateur - British Amateur sweep.
- Unheralded Tony Manero closes with a 67 to win the U.S. Open with a record 282.
- In winning the U.S. Amateur, Johnny Fischer

is the last to capture a national championship using hickory-shafted clubs.

1938

- A new USGA rule limits players to 14 clubs. Some players (e.g., Lawson Little) have been carrying as many as 25. The Rule is designed to restore shot-making skill.
- Ralph Guldahl wins his second consecutive U.S. Open.
- Patty Berg, twice a runner-up, wins the U.S. Women's Amateur at age 20.

1939

- Byron Nelson wins the U.S. Open in a playoff over Craig Wood and Denny Shute after Sam Snead makes an eight on the 72nd hole.

1940

- The Walker Cup is canceled because of the war.
- Ed "Porky" Oliver would have tied for first place in the U.S. Open, but he is disqualified from the playoff. Oliver and five other players start the final round before their scheduled starting times due to an oncoming storm. Lawson Little defeats Gene Sarazen for the title.

1941

- Craig Wood ends a string of frustrating runner-up finishes in major events by winning both The Masters and the U.S. Open.
- The USGA develops a machine for testing golf-ball velocity at impact. Plans for limiting initial velocity are put on hold until after the war.

1942

- A Rule change authorizes players to stop play on their own initiative if they consider themselves endangered by lightning.
- The USGA cancels all its championships for the duration of the war as the U.S. government halts the manufacturing of golf equipment.
- Ben Hogan wins the Hale America National Open, a charity event for the Navy Relief Fund and the USO. He shoots a second-round 62 en route to a 17-under-par total.

1946

- The first U.S. Women's Open is held, the only one ever conducted at match play. Patty Berg is the champion.

1947

- The USGA revises and simplifies *The Rules of Golf*, reducing 61 Rules to 21. The R&A doesn't go along, however.
- The U.S. Open is televised — but only locally — on KSD-TV in St. Louis.

1948

- The first U.S. Junior Amateur is played, with Dean Lind beating future U.S. Open champion Ken Venturi in the championship final.
- Ben Hogan captures the first of four U.S. Opens with a record score of 276.
- *Golf Journal* magazine — originally titled *USGA Journal Combining Timely Turf Topics*— appears.

1949

- Marlene Bauer, 15, wins the inaugural U.S. Girls' Junior Championship, and turns pro later in the year.
- Louise Suggs wins the U.S. Women's Open by 14 strokes.

1950

- Ben Hogan returns to The Tour a year after nearly being killed in an automobile accident and wins the U.S. Open at Merion in an 18-hole playoff.
- Babe Zaharias wins the U.S. Women's Open by nine strokes.

1951

- The USGA and R&A hold a joint conference and after agree on uniform Rules of Golf worldwide. The rules go into effect the following year. The only remaining difference is the size of the ball (the R&A permits a diameter of 1.62 inches compared to the USGA's 1.68 inches). The stymie is abolished, center-shafted putters are legalized (in Great Britain, center-shafted putters had been illegal since 1909), and the out-of-bounds penalty is made stroke and distance.
- Ben Hogan wins a second consecutive U.S. Open at Oakland Hills, deemed a "monster"

after its redesign by Robert Trent Jones Sr. in 1950.

1952
• Julius Boros captures the U.S. Open.

1953
• Ben Hogan takes the three major events he enters — The Masters, U.S. Open and British Open championships. It is his fourth U.S. Open title.

1954
• The U.S. Open is televised nationally for the first time. Also new—the holes are roped for gallery control.
• Babe Zaharias wins the U.S. Women's Open by 12 strokes one year after cancer surgery.

1955
• Unheralded Jack Fleck stuns Ben Hogan with his U.S. Open playoff win at The Olympic Club in San Francisco, CA.

1956
• Cary Middlecoff captures his second U.S. Open title.
• Yardages for guidance in computing par are increased to current levels:

> Three — up to 250 yards
> Four — 251 to 470 yards
> Five — more than 470 yards

1957
• Jackie Pung finishes as the apparent winner of the U.S. Women's Open, but is disqualified for signing an incorrect scorecard. Betsy Rawls takes the title.

1958
• At the age of 23, Mickey Wright sweeps the U.S. Women's Open and LPGA Championships.
• The USGA and R&A jointly organize the World Amateur Golf Council and conduct the first World Amateur Team Championship at the Old Course in St. Andrews, Scotland. Bob Jones serves as captain of the American squad.

1959
• Mickey Wright wins her second consecutive U.S. Women's Open.
• Bill Wright becomes the first African-American player to win a national championship when he takes the U.S. Amateur Public Links.
• Nineteen-year-old Jack Nicklaus captures the first of two U.S. Amateur titles.

1960
• Arnold Palmer has his greatest year. He wins The Masters with birdies on the last two holes and the U.S. Open with a final-round 65.
• Betsy Rawls wins her fourth U.S. Women's Open.

1961
• Mickey Wright wins three majors — the U.S. Women's Open, LPGA Championship, and the Titleholders—and 10 events in all.
• Anne Quast Sander wins the U.S. Women's Amateur by a record 14-and-13 margin over Phyllis Preuss.

1962
• Rookie professional Jack Nicklaus beats home-town favorite Arnold Palmer to win the U.S. Open in a playoff at Oakmont Country Club near Pittsburgh, PA.
• For the first time, water hazards are marked with painted lines at the U.S. Open.

1964
• Ken Venturi wins the U.S. Open despite suffering from heat prostration during a 36-hole final day at Congressional Country Club.
• Mickey Wright wins her fourth U.S. Open, one of 11 tournaments she captures during the year.

1965
• The U.S. Amateur changes from match play to stroke play. The U.S. Open is held over four days instead of three.
• Gary Player becomes the third player in history to win all four majors when he captures the U.S. Open. The South African is the first foreigner to win the Open in 45 years. He donates his winner's check to the USGA in support of junior golf.

1966
• Billy Casper wins the U.S. Open in a playoff after Arnold Palmer drops a seven-stroke lead over the last nine holes of regulation at The Olympic Club in San Francisco, CA.

1967
• Jack Nicklaus takes the U.S. Open with a record total of 275 at Baltusrol Golf Club in Springfield, NJ.
• Catherine Lacoste of France becomes the only amateur to win the U.S. Women's Open.

1968
• Croquet-style putting, recently employed by Sam Snead, is ruled illegal by the USGA.
• Lee Trevino is the first player to break 70 for all four rounds in a U.S. Open, winning with a record-tying 275 total.
• JoAnne Gunderson Carner wins her fifth U.S. Women's Amateur.

1970
• England's Tony Jacklin wins the U.S. Open.
• Lanny Wadkins beats Tom Kite by one stroke to win the U.S. Amateur.

1971
• Lee Trevino becomes the first player to win the U.S., British, and Canadian Opens with three victories in a four-week stretch. Tiger Woods would match that feat in 2000.
• Astronaut Alan Shepard hits a 6-iron shot during a walk on the moon. He later donates the club to the USGA Museum.

1972
• Jack Nicklaus wins The Masters and U.S. Open, but then is thwarted in his bid for the Grand Slam by Lee Trevino in the British Open.
• Carolyn Cudone wins her fifth consecutive USGA Senior Women's Amateur, a record for any USGA event.

1973
• Johnny Miller becomes the U.S. Open champion, firing a record 63 in the final round at Oakmont.
• The U.S. Amateur returns to match play; the winner is Craig Stadler.

1974

- Sandra Haynie sweeps the U.S. Women's Open and LPGA Championships.

1976

- The USGA adopts the Overall Distance Standard for golf balls, limiting distance to 280 yards under standard test conditions.

1977

- The U.S. Open is the first American golf event to provide television coverage of all 18 holes.

1979

- The USGA plants a tree overnight at Inverness Club in Toledo, OH to block a short-cut taken by several players in the first round of the U.S. Open.

1980

- Jack Nicklaus captures the U.S. Open (his fourth) and PGA Championship (his fifth) at age 40. He shoots a U.S. Open record 272 in the Open at Baltusrol and ties the 18-hole record with a 63.
- The USGA adds the U.S. Senior Open to its list of championships. Roberto De Vicenzo is the inaugural champion.
- The USGA introduces the golf ball Symmetry Standard to the *Rules of Golf*.

1981

- The USGA adds the U.S. Mid-Amateur Championship for players 25 and older, an event in which career amateurs won't have to face college golfers.

1982

- Tom Watson takes his only U.S. Open, chipping in on the 71st hole to beat Jack Nicklaus at Pebble Beach.
- Juli Inkster wins her third consecutive U.S. Women's Amateur, the first to accomplish this feat in 48 years.

1984

- Hollis Stacy claims her third U.S. Women's Open to go with her three U. S. Girls' Junior titles.

1985

- The USGA introduces the Slope System to adjust handicaps according to the difficulty of the course being played.
- T.C. Chen drops a four-stroke lead in the U.S. Open at Oakland Hills by double-hitting a chip shot and making a quadruple bogey on the fifth hole. Andy North wins.

1986

- Forty-three-year-old Ray Floyd wins the U.S. Open at Shinnecock Hills, the first Open played at the club in 90 years.

1987

- Judy Bell becomes the first woman elected to the USGA Executive Committee.

1988

- The USGA rules that Ping Eye2 irons don't conform to the Rules because the grooves are too close together. Karsten Manufacturing, maker of Ping, files suit. A settlement will be reached in 1990 under which new Pings are modified to conform and existing Pings are deemed acceptable.

1989

- Curtis Strange wins his second consecutive U.S. Open, the first to do so since Ben Hogan (1950 and 1951).

1990

- Hale Irwin, at age 45, becomes the oldest U.S. Open winner.
- Phil Mickelson sweeps the U.S. Amateur and NCAA Championship, a feat not accomplished since Jack Nicklaus in 1961.
- The R&A adopts the American-sized ball (1.68 inches) as the standard all over the world.

1991

- Payne Stewart claims the U.S. Open at Hazeltine National Golf Club in Chaska, MN in a playoff with Scott Simpson.

1992

- John F. Merchant, a Connecticut attorney, is the first African American elected to the USGA Executive Committee.

1993

- For the third consecutive year, Tiger Woods is the U.S. Junior Amateur champion. No other player has accomplished this feat.
- Sarah LeBrun Ingram becomes the first player to take the U.S. Women's Mid-Amateur Championship twice.

1994

- Arnold Palmer bids farewell to the U.S. Open in a stirring march up the 18th fairway at Oakmont.
- Patty Sheehan wins the U.S. Women's Open at Indianwood Golf and Country Club in Huron, MI, her second victory in three years.

1995

- Corey Pavin claims the U.S. Open during the USGA's Centennial.
- Tiger Woods wins his second consecutive U.S. Amateur Championship held at Newport Country Club.

1996

- Judy Bell becomes the first woman elected president of the USGA.
- Tiger Woods wins his third consecutive U.S. Amateur Championship at Pumpkin Ridge Golf Club in North Pines, OR. Later, he joins the PGA Tour, wins twice, and earns Rookie of the Year honors.
- Kelli Kuehne wins her second consecutive U.S. Women's Amateur title, and later adds the British Ladies Open Amateur.
- Annika Sorenstam wins her second consecutive Women's Open, held at Pine Needles Golf Resort in Southern Pines, NC.

1997

- Ernie Els wins the U.S. Open at Congressional, his second in four years.
- Jack Nicklaus competes in the U.S. Open at Congressional — his 150th consecutive major championship.

1998

- Lee Janzen wins his second U.S. Open title of the 1990s at The Olympic Club.
- Casey Martin rides in a golf cart at the U.S. Open.

- Se Ri Pak, a 19-year-old from South Korea, captivates the LPGA Tour with major wins at the U.S. Women's Open and the LPGA Championships.

1999
- Thirteen-year-old Aree Wongluekiet becomes the youngest winner in USGA history by capturing the Girls' Junior at Green Spring Valley Hunt Club in Owings Mills, MD.
- The U.S. Senior Open attracts record crowds of more than 250,000 in Des Moines, IA.
- Payne Stewart wins his second U.S. Open title at Pinehurst, sinking a dramatic par putt on the 72nd hole. Tragically, he is killed, along with five others, in a plane crash four months later.
- Juli Inkster smashes the U.S. Women's Open scoring record at Old Waverly Golf Club in West Point, MS.
- The USGA implements testing protocol for "spring-like" effect in metal woods.

2000
- The USGA celebrates the 100th playing of the U.S. Open, U.S. Amateur, and U.S. Women's Amateur, as well as the 75th playing of the U.S. Amateur Public Links.
- Shigeki Maruyama cards a 58 in sectional qualifying for the U.S. Open.
- At 10 years of age, Michelle Wie becomes the youngest player to compete in a USGA women's amateur competition when she qualifies for the Women's Amateur Public Links in Aberdeen, NC.
- Tiger Woods rolls to a record 15-stroke victory at the U.S. Open at Pebble Beach. It is Woods' first Open title and his seventh USGA championship. He would go on to win the season's final two major championships, the British Open at St. Andrews and the PGA Championship at Valhalla, becoming the first golfer since Ben Hogan in 1953 to win three majors in a single year.
- By defeating Anna Schultz, 3 and 2, in the final of the Women's Mid-Amateur, Ellen Port becomes only the second player in the championship's history to win three Women's Mid-Amateur titles, joining Sarah LeBrun Ingram.

2001
- Retief Goosen wins the U.S. Open at Southern Hills Country Club in Tulsa, OK in a playoff over Mark Brooks.
- Karrie Webb rolls to an eight-shot victory at the U.S. Women's Open at Pine Needles and joins six others as back-to-back winners of this championship.
- Christina Kim registers the lowest 18-hole score in any USGA championship when she fires a 62 in the second round of stroke-play qualifying at the U.S. Girls' Junior at Indian Hills Country Club in Mission Hills, KS.
- James Vargas establishes a U.S. Junior 36-hole stroke-play scoring record of 132 at Oak Hills Country Club in San Antonio, TX.
- Meredith Duncan outlasts Nicole Perrot in a 37-hole thriller for the U.S. Women's Amateur title at Flint Hills National Golf Club in Wichita, KS. The loss prevented Perrot from becoming the first golfer to capture the U.S. Girl's Junior and Women's Amateur in the same year.
- In the first 36-hole final in U.S. Mid-Amateur history, Tim Jackson defeats George Zahringer, 1 up, at San Joaquin Country Club in Fresno, CA.
- The Great Britain and Ireland Walker Cup team registers a 15–9 victory over the USA squad at Ocean Forest Golf Club in Sea Island, GA. It's the first time the Great Britain & Ireland squad posted consecutive victories over the USA in the 79-year history of the Match.
- By winning the USGA Senior Amateur crown at Norwood Hills Country Club in St. Louis, MO, Kemp Richardson made he and his father, John Richardson, the only father-son duo to capture USGA championships. The elder Richardson had won the Senior Amateur title in 1987.

2002
- For the first time ever, the U.S. Open is held at a publicly owned facility (Bethpage State Park's Black Course in Farmingdale, NY). Tiger Woods is the only player to finish under par (-3).
- Juli Inkster returns to the site of her first Women's Amateur championship (Prairie Dunes Country Club in Hutchinson, KS) and fires a final-round 66 to beat Annika Sorenstam by two strokes for her second U.S. Women's Open title.

- Carol Semple Thompson, playing in her record 12th Curtis Cup Match, sinks a 27-foot birdie putt from the fringe at the 18th hole to secure the USA's 11–7 victory over GB&I. The dramatic putt was fitting since the Match was played near Thompson's hometown of Pittsburgh at the Fox Chapel Golf Club.
- George Zahringer, at 49, becomes the oldest player to win the U.S. Mid-Amateur title when he defeats Jerry Courville Jr., 3 and 2, at his home course, The Stanwich Club in Greenwich, CT.
- Carol Semple Thompson, en route to winning her fourth consecutive USGA Senior Women's Amateur Championship at Mid-Pines Inn and Golf Club in Southern Pines, NC, establishes a consecutive match-play winning streak record of 24.

2003
- Michelle Wie, 13, becomes the youngest champion of an adult USGA championship when she defeats Virada Nirapathponporn in the final of the Women's Amateur Public Links Championship at Ocean Hammock Golf Club in Palm Coast, FL.
- Jim Furyk establishes a 54-hole U.S. Open scoring record of 200 en route to a three-stroke victory over Stephen Leaney. Furyk's 72-hole total of 272 tied an Open mark held by Jack Nicklaus, Lee Janzen and Tiger Woods.
- Hilary Lunke outlasts Angela Stanford and Kelly Robbins in a playoff for the U.S. Women's Open title. Lunke becomes the first player since Annika Sorenstam in 1995 to make the Women's Open her first professional victory. Lunke also is the first champion to have won by going through local and sectional qualifying.

2004
- Ryan Moore completes a remarkable amateur season, winning the U.S. Amateur and U.S. Amateur Public Links championships, as well as the Western Amateur and the NCAA Division I Golf Championship individual title. He was also the low scorer for the USA, who won the World Amateur Team Championship.
- Retief Goosen wins his second U.S. Open championship in difficult final round conditions at Shinnecock Hills.
- Sihwan Kim, 15, becomes the second-

youngest champion in U.S. Junior Amateur history, defeating David Chung, 14, at The Olympic Club.

2005
- Michael Campbell becomes the first player from New Zealand to win the U.S. Open, defeating Tiger Woods by two strokes at Pinehurst No. 2.
- Korea's Birdie Kim holes an improbable shot from a greenside bunker on the final hole of the Women's Open at Cherry Hills, securing a two-stroke victory.
- Michelle Wie, 15, advances to the quarterfinals of the U.S. Amateur Public Links at Shaker Run Golf Club in Lebanon, OH, becoming the first woman to compete in a traditionally male USGA championship.
- Kevin Tway, son of PGA Tour player Bob Tway, triumphs in the U.S. Junior Amateur Championship.
- Allen Doyle shoots 63 in the final round of the U.S. Senior Open at NCR Country Club, near Dayton, OH, coming from nine strokes off the lead to claim his first individual USGA championship title.
- Morgan Pressel wins the U.S. Women's Amateur at Ansley Golf Club near Atlanta, GA
- Italy's Edoardo Molinari wins the U.S. Amateur at Merion Golf Club, becoming the first Italian to win the championship.

A gathering of U.S. Open champions at Pebble Beach to commemorate the 100th anniversary of the championship.

2006

- Tadd Fujikawa, 15, becomes the youngest competitor in U.S. Open history when he plays in the first round at Winged Foot Golf Club in Mamaroneck, NY. Australia's Geoff Ogilvy wins the championship.
- Michelle Wie becomes the first woman in history to win a local qualifier for the U.S. Open, and then becomes the first to play in U.S. Open sectional qualifying. She shoots 68–75 at Canoe Brook Country Club in Summit, NJ but

falls short by five strokes.

- Loren Roberts shoots 62 in the third round of the U.S. Senior Open at Prairie Dunes Country Club—the lowest score ever recorded in any USGA open championship. Defending champion Allen Doyle repeats his title, dueling Kansas native and local favorite Tom Watson over the closing holes.
- Scotland's Richie Ramsay wins the U.S. Amateur at Hazeltine National Golf Club, becoming the first Scotsman since Findlay

Douglas in 1898 to win the championship. Billy Horschel, a sophomore at the University of Florida, shoots 60 at Chaska Town Course in the first round of stroke play, setting a record for the lowest single-round score in any USGA championship.

CLASSIC SHOTS
THE GREATEST IMAGES FROM THE
UNITED STATES GOLF ASSOCIATION
Marty Parkes

Published by the National Geographic Society

John M. Fahey, Jr., President and Chief Executive Officer

Gilbert M. Grosvenor, Chairman of the Board

Nina D. Hoffman, Executive Vice President;
   President, Books Publishing Group

Prepared by the Book Division

Kevin Mulroy, Senior Vice President and Publisher

Leah Bendavid-Val, Director of Photography Publishing
   and Illustrations

Marianne R. Koszorus, Director of Design

Barbara Brownell Grogan, Executive Editor

Elizabeth Newhouse, Director of Travel Publishing

Carl Mehler, Director of Maps

Staff for this Book

Ellen Beal, Editor

Christopher A. Liedel, Consulting Editor

Dana Chivvis, Illustrations Editor

Cinda Rose, Art Director

Mike Horenstein, Production Project Manager

Jennifer Thornton, Managing Editor

Sanaa Akkach, Assistant Designer

Gary Colbert, Production Director

Marshall Kiker, Illustrations Specialist

USGA Staff for this Book

Marty Parkes, Senior Director of Communications

Rand Jerris, Director of USGA Museum and Archives

John Mummert, Senior Staff Photographer and Manager
   of USGA Photo Archives

Corinne Felice, Senior Administrative Assistant

Ellie Kaiser, Photo Editing Liaison

Jaime Mikle, Photo Archives Fulfillment Liaison

Manufacturing and Quality Management

Christopher A. Liedel, Chief Financial Officer

Phillip L. Schlosser, Vice President

John T. Dunn, Technical Director

Vincent P. Ryan, Director

Chris Brown, Director

Maryclare Tracy, Manager

FOUNDED IN 1888, the National Geographic Society
is one of the largest nonprofit scientific and educa-
tional organizations in the world. It reaches more than
285 million people worldwide each month through its
official journal, NATIONAL GEOGRAPHIC, and its four
other magazines; the National Geographic Channel;
television docmentaries; radio programs; films; books;
videos and DVDs; maps; and interactive media.
National Geographic has funded more than 8,000 scientific research projects and supports an education
program combating geograpic illiteracy. For more
information, please call 1-800-NGS LINE (647-5463)
or write to the following address:

National Geographic Society
1145 17th Street N.W.
Washington, D.C. 20036-4688 U.S.A.

Visit us online at www.nationalgeographic.com/books.

The United States Golf Association (USGA) has
served as the national governing body of golf since its
formation in 1894. It is a non-proft organization run by
golfers for the benefit of golfers. The USGA remains
committed to promoting policies and programs For the
Good of the Game.

To find out more, please contact:
USGA, Golf House
77 Liberty Corner Road
P.O. Box 708
Far Hills, NJ 07931

Visit us online at www.usga.org.

Library of Congress Cataloging-in-Publication Data
available upon request.

ISBN-10: 1-4262-0038-2
ISBN-13: 978-1-4262-0038-0

Printed in U.S.A.